THE LETTER KILLS
BUT THE SPIRIT GIVES LIFE

THE LETTER KILLS
BUT THE SPIRIT GIVES LIFE

*The Smiths -- Abolitionists,
Suffragists, Bible Translators*

KATHLEEN L. HOUSLEY

THE HISTORICAL SOCIETY OF GLASTONBURY, CONNECTICUT

Library of Congress Cataloging in Publication Data
Housley, Kathleen.
        The Letter Kills But the Spirit Gives Life.

        Bibliography: p
        Includes index.

        1. Family -- United States -- History -- 19th Century
        2. Bible -- Translating
        3. Women's Rights -- History -- United States
        4. United States -- Biography

ISBN: 0-9610676-2-4

Printed by the Historical Society of Glastonbury
1944 Main Street
Glastonbury, CT. 06033

Printed on acid-free paper.

For Timothy, Marc and William
for their unflagging support and patience

Contents

ACKNOWLEDGEMENTS

Although I owe thanks to numerous archivists, curators and librarians for their assistance in locating source material for this book, I am indebted to Doris Armstead, librarian of the Historical Society of Glastonbury, and Marjorie G. McNulty, historian for the Town of Glastonbury, for their invaluable help and guidance. I would also like to thank Olive Rhines, a former member of the Historical Society of Glastonbury, who translated Julia Smith's diary from French for the years 1810 through 1825. It is just such arduous and often unsung work which these three women have done which makes the preservation and study of history possible. I would also like to thank Dr. Margaret Carey-Best at Wesleyan University for her suggestions and guidance on my Masters thesis which was the basis for this book. Dr. Frank Kirkpatrick at Trinity College was most helpful in reviewing the material on Sandemanianism and Millerism and providing me with bibliographical guidance.

Psalm I

Happy the man who went not in the counsel of the unjust, and he stood not in the way of the sinful, and sat not in the seat of those scoffing.

2 But his delight is in the law of Jehovah, and in his law he will meditate day and night.

3 And he was as a tree planted by the streams of water which will give its fruit in its time; his leaf shall not fall away, and all which he shall do shall be prospered.

4 Not so the unjust: but as the chaff which the wind shall drive away.

5 For this, the unjust shall not rise up in judgment, and the sinful in the assembly of the just.

6 For Jehovah shall know the way of the just: but the way of the unjust shall perish.

The Holy Bible,
Translated by Julia E. Smith

INTRODUCTION

Social evils are always present, vice is always in the saddle while virtue trudges on afoot. Not merely the existence of evil but the recognition of it is the prerequisite for reform.

David Donald
"Toward a Reconsideration of Abolition"

On a farm that sloped gently from the eastern hills down across the flood plain to the Connecticut River there lived during the nineteenth century a family of fierce intelligence with the prosaic name of Smith. To offset such a common surname, the father and mother named their five daughters Hancy Zephina, Cyrinthia Sacretia, Laurilla Aleroyla, Julia Evelina, and Abby Hadassah. Just as the intricacy of their first names countered the plainness of their last, so the complexity of their intellectual lives countered the parochialism of Glastonbury, the Connecticut village in which they dwelt. It was in making their town the laughingstock of a nation that Julia and Abby first won their fame and, in the process, brought a little levity into the stern self-righteousness of the women's suffrage movement. But from that levity also sprang serious proof that women were clearly the intellectual equals of men, for Julia became the first woman ever to translate and publish the Bible in its entirety.

The notorious event that started it all took place when Julia and Abby, the two remaining sisters, were eighty and seventy-five years old -- quiescent ages for most people, when political activism is something about which to reminisce. Discovering in 1872 that the Glastonbury town fathers had increased the assessment on their land and on that of two widows but had not increased the assessment on land belonging to males, the sisters sounded the battle cry issued one hundred years earlier and charged that they were the victims of taxation without representation. Deaf to their complaints, the town tax collector seized the sisters' seven Alderney cows -- named Jessie, Daisy, Whitey, Minnie, Proxy, Bessie, and Lily -- and auctioned them off for back taxes. The next time taxes were due, the collector seized eleven acres of prime meadow worth $200 per acre and sold the land to cover a tax of $49.83. This imperious treatment so infuriated the sisters that they filed suit, fighting their case all the way up to the State Supreme Court, thereby drawing the attention of national suffrage leaders, including Susan B. Anthony, Lucy Stone, and Elizabeth Cady Stanton. Meanwhile the cows came to the attention of newspaper editors all across the country who saw in them a symbol as potent as chests of tea floating in Boston harbor.

As the incident with the cows reveals, the Smiths lived physically in the nineteenth century while leaning mentally toward the twentieth. Had there been but one Smith, exclusion and ridicule would have been that person's societal lot, but there were seven -- enough to form a private society fostering mutual support. No matter how the community felt about their determined stands on issues such as abolition of slavery and the nature of religion, no matter how prolonged and bitter the battle about taxation without representation, the Smiths prevailed because they found strength in each other.

But none of this explains why the Smiths became activists in the first place. From whence came the impulse for social reform? In his ground-breaking essay on the nature of the abolitionist movement, "Toward a Reconsideration of Abolition," David Donald stated that whenever a practice which has been around for century upon century suddenly receives the critical moral attention of an increasingly large segment of a society, the immediate cause of the concern is not the evil inherent in the practice itself. Slavery had been in existence for millennia, yet there was no major movement to abolish it until the late eighteenth century, and not until the nineteenth century did public opposition become widespread. According to Donald's thesis, some other factor had to be at work when abolition began, since the "evil" of slavery was obviously not "inherent." The same can be said for women's rights. Although there were individual voices calling for greater freedom prior to the Revolutionary War, a "movement" did not begin until the nineteenth century.

Underscoring Donald's key word "recognition," it is here that a study of the Smith family of Glastonbury, Connecticut, may be useful. They became deeply involved in every major social cause of the nineteenth century though only women's suffrage touched them personally. They never owned a slave and never saw the South, yet they were ardent abolitionists. There was no alcoholism in their family, yet the temperance movement received their full support. All five daughters were born near the end of the eighteenth century of highly intellectual parents. None of the daughters married or moved away from home except for Julia who married for the first time at age 87 after her last sister had died and she was lost in loneliness. As a result, there is a constancy about the family which helps reveal how they became involved in social causes, albeit from the sidelines. However, a caveat is in order: there is the ever present danger in biography of placing too much meaning on the actions of one particular individual or, in this case, family and, as a result, overemphasizing their impact on larger historical processes.

Yet with this warning in mind, a close look at the Smiths is very revealing because within the confines of propriety they pushed for change. Only during the battle with the Town of Glastonbury over taxation without representation did Julia and Abby dare to confront physically an injustice and risk both their reputation and their property in the process. The tax battle was for the Smiths the last stand because they thought that they would soon die of old age and, therefore, they had nothing to lose but life itself, which was already tenuous. The historian should not ignore these women because their efforts to achieve justice were carried on with the pen and were often fruitless. In the long run, the causes for which they fought so hard did prevail: the slaves were freed and women won the vote. But just as they were disappointed by the slowness to give men and women of African descent full human rights following their emancipation by President Abraham Lincoln, so it can be presumed that the Smiths, had they lived, would have been disappointed with the slowness of change following the winning of suffrage for women. For them individual freedom was like a butterfly that flitted ever further away. Its attainment was less important than the attempt to keep it in sight.

Notes on Sources

Julia Smith kept a diary from 1810 to 1842 in French. The diary has been translated up through 1825 in its entirety by Olive Rhines, a member of the Historical Society of Glastonbury. Short sections of the rest have been translated by Mary Helen Kidder. Julia also kept a diary in English, mostly of meteorological entries from 1842 to 1854. Both diaries are in the archives of the Connecticut Historical Society in Hartford. The translation is in the archives of the Historical Society of Glastonbury.

Hannah Hickok Smith's diary is extant for the last six years of her life, July 1844 to 1850. It is in the Connecticut State Library in Hartford, along with an account book from 1821-24. A small selection of letters, principally from the Smiths to Hannah's mother Abigail Hickok Mitchel, who lived in South Britain, Connecticut, are also in the Connecticut State Library.

David Hicock's diary for 1769 and 1770 is owned by the Historical Society of Glastonbury. His diary for 1771 through 1783 is owned by the Connecticut State Library. It covers all of 1771, then has occasional entries for 1775, 1776, 1778 and 1783. Both diaries may be transcriptions made by Hannah.

Letters and papers including the drafts of the anti-slavery petitions and suffrage material are owned by the Historical Society of Glastonbury. These include a small sketchbook of Laurilla Smith, and some of Hannah's translations. Copies of the following three books which Julia published are in several libraries and archives including the Historical Society of Glastonbury, the Connecticut Historical Society, and the Connecticut State Library: *Abby Smith and Her Cows*, a book comprised chiefly of newspaper clippings about their suffrage battle with the Town of Glastonbury; *Mother's Poems*, a collection of Hannah's poetry; and *The Holy Bible*. Julia's handwritten translations of the *Bible* are in the Connecticut Historical Society. Olin Library at Wesleyan University owns a King James Version of the Bible which Julia interlined with inks of different colors.

Other records and diaries were also consulted including the Glassenbury [sic] Town Book, which contains the records of town meetings etc., the diary of Joseph Wright, a Glastonbury farmer who lived at the same time as the Smiths, and the archives of St. Luke's Episcopal Church and First Church of Christ Congregational in Glastonbury. Many individual letters are scattered among libraries and archives across the country. Most pertain to the tax battle and the publication of the Bible since these two events created national interest. Because of the commonness of the name Smith, and the fact that there were more than one Hannah Smith, Abby Smith and Julia Smith alive during this period, research is arduous and results in many false leads.

I have relied as little as possible on obituaries and memoirs written after the death of the last sister. By then, the Smith women were creatures of legend, some of which they helped spread themselves at the end of their lives in order to give greater weight to their suffrage demands. Whenever I have quoted a memoir in this paper, I have tried to corroborate the information with another source, preferably primary, not secondary.

"And he was as a tree planted
by the streams of water."
Psalm 1:3

1

HANNAH HADASSAH HICKOK:

A TREE PLANTED BY STREAMS OF WATER

Born on August 7, 1767 in South Britain, Connecticut, Hannah Hadassah Hickok was the only child of David Hickok and Abigail Johnson, who were, at the time of her birth, thirty and twenty eight years old respectively. As a young man, David had attended Yale College apparently in the hopes of becoming a minister but was forced to quit due to illness. He returned to South Britain, an area made up of steep hills and narrow valleys through which the Pomperaug River meandered peacefully before flowing into the much larger Housatonic River. Here he married Abigail Johnson, a respected weaver who sold linen, wool and felt to families in the area, a job with which David sometimes helped and which would also become part of Hannah's childhood. On March 23, 1770, David wrote in his diary:

> Wove 7 yards and wound 2 wrun [sic] on
> Quills - finished weaving a Piece of Linnen
> [sic] containing 20 yards - 5 1/4 yards for
> John Cowel & 14 3/4 for Vefter Wooster at
> 6 pr. yard...A beggar came to my House
> today drefs in mens clothing to whom I gave
> an old woolen shirt, some people supposed
> he was a woman -- I measured a basket of
> corn for my Pigs - a cold day for the
> Season.

Clearly, the union of an educated farmer and teacher with a talented weaver who possessed a measure of financial independence, was propitious to the raising of a single, intelligent, and individualistic daughter. Until she died at age 83 on December 27, 1850, Hannah would remember her childhood as one of the happiest, most free times of her life. With deep longing she would reminisce about galloping side-saddle through thunderstorms, exploring hidden glades curtained with vines, and studying in the quiet of her own room undisturbed by the bustle of guests. Raised in the period prior to and during the Revolutionary War, she absorbed a spirit of independence which would never be squelched, although it would certainly be constricted. Upon reaching adulthood following the War, she found herself immediately caught up in a period of enormous national change which, paradoxically, would bring about restrictions on the roles women could play. The Smith family's ardent involvement with abolition, temperance, and suffrage can be traced in part to Hannah's personal experience of freedom in her childhood and its intolerable loss in her adulthood.

During the winter months when the demands of farming decreased and there was time in the evening for more intellectual pursuits, David put his Yale education to use and taught school.

> 18 Monday [December 1769] began school
> at Bullet hill had 13 scholars/in the evening
> went to Singing meeting at Pam
> Wheelers/my wife finished weaving a piece
> of flannel for John Tiff of 24 yrds. at 6
> [illegible mark] per yard.

Two years later the evening school was moved from Bullet Hill in Southbury to the Hickok home. Night settled early on the thin days of winter, and with it settled the cold through which the bundled children walked to class, drawn by the light beckoning through frosted windows. Hanging up their woolen coats and caps on wooden pegs, they settled in front of the fireplace to learn how to shape their letters with quill pens, and to cipher, often working the sums in charcoal or chalk on boards, paper being very dear and not something to waste on practice exercises. While the flames from candles and hearth made shadows dance across their faces, the children also learned to read from the Bible -- the omnipresent book in the Protestant homes of their parents.

On January 3, 1771, David noted in his diary that he had 43 scholars of whom only seven came to the first class. The salary was "a penny a Scholar per Night" which was paid at the end of the session by the Congregational Church in South Britain, a church which David had been instrumental in forming just a few years before. Two months later he listed 45 students, of whom 29 were white males and were set down in his diary as "scholars," 17 were women, and one was a black male, listed as "Peter a negro." Of that number, 38 students made it through the entire four months. Sometimes snowstorms or extreme cold prevented the children from getting to school; attendance fluctuated markedly, probably due to sickness and chores. Finally, classes ended completely at the end of April when the daylight lengthened and intensified and the demands of farm life began to increase sharply for both students and teacher. Formal learning was a luxury borne of winter, when darkness and cold allowed farm children a certain degree of idleness. When seedtime arrived, learning had to be shelved, along with the books, to wait again for the short end of the year.

Although during this period it was common for the Congregational minister to serve the triple functions of religious leader, civic leader, and school master, David Hickok was so well regarded as a non-ordained educator that he was hired in 1774 by the neighboring church district of Southbury to keep a "high school" apparently for teenagers. When spring came, the family moved the short distance east to Southbury and lived there nine months in the house of Eliazer Knowles. That summer when Hannah turned seven, her mother taught her to spin wool, a time-consuming task essential to her mother's craft. She was also responsible for taking care of the flock of ducks, a job which she shared with a friend named Pata Sheds.

As is already apparent, both David and Abigail were deeply religious. David was one of the founders of the Congregational Society in South Britain which constructed its first meeting house in 1770, the year Hannah turned three. According to *Contributions of the Ecclesiastical History of Connecticut*, the "church in South Britain came off from the church in Southbury about the year 1769, and were allowed what was called winter privileges." This meant that it was too hard for the members to attend the Southbury church in the wintertime given the distance, the weather, and the poor road conditions; therefore, they were granted permission to establish their own church which would meet during the winter months only. The members were expected to return to the Southbury Church when the improving spring weather made the roads passable again. However, it seems that South Britain quickly established itself as a four-season church totally separate from Southbury.

Along with frequent notations about farming and weaving, David often noted in his diary the topic of Rev. Jehu Minor's sermon as well as the scripture which had been read. As an old woman, Hannah recalled attending "singing meetings" at the church with her friend Phebe Mitchel and cousin Belleria Hinman, whom Hannah called affectionately "Bella." At these "meetings" hymns were the centerpiece of worship instead of a sermon. Although decidedly religious, these meetings had a pleasant social aspect. The church in South Britain, as was true in agrarian communities throughout New England and indeed most of the Colonies, was the cultural nucleus of the little community. Religion was not confined to Sunday mornings but suffused the entire week. For a woman who would in time be caught up in radical theological torrents, Hannah's religious upbringing was definitely a conservative pool of still waters.

In 1776 when Hannah was nine years old, the Revolutionary War touched their lives, albeit in a minor way. David Hickok wrote on October 27, 1776 that "there was a muster of every able-bodied male to march to Stamford." Whether because of his age of 39 or because of some infirmity, he did not go. The next day he noted that besides tending his oxen, cutting wood and drawing stone, he could hear the cannon. "Mr. Reynolds just came from the army and says they had a very hot Battle at the white plains yesterday." White Plains, New York, was approximately 25 miles to the southwest of South Britain. The battle, which the Continental Army lost, meant that Manhattan and Long Island were firmly in the hands of the

British and that towns along the Sound and in Fairfield County were especially vulnerable to attack. Seven days later on November 4, 1776, David wrote "Daniel Downs, Amasa Garrit are killed and John Chilfon had his arm shot off in the Battle of the white plains -- a Soldier Belonging to Boston Government Lodged at my House this night to whom I sold my old watch."

Though not touching on their lives physically, the Revolutionary War touched the Hickoks economically, as it did everyone, because the Colonies had relied heavily on England for many household items including glass and fine cloth, as well as powder, cannon and other types of military supplies. When Hannah was 79 years old, she reminisced in her diary about those years:

> I have seen children's frocks pinned with thorns, I have seen wooden tea cups & saucers in some families, but we could spin & weave our own garments. Happy were the daughters whose mothers had laid by a gown or two of silk & callico [sic] or chintz. My mother had a comfortable number altered for me when I was in my fifteenth year. The war did not end till I was near 16, when we began to buy, tho' cloth of all kinds was dear.

Raw cotton used to weave calico and chintz was imported principally from the West Indies through the ports of New York and Boston. During the war it was considered as much a luxury as silk. In fact, according to Hannah, a calico dress was "a grand affair kept choice to wear only to meeting and taken off as soon as we returned till I was 15. At 16 peace was proclaimed and my mother bought, I think two gowns." That year Hannah also cut her hair "short" because it was "fashionable." (By "short" she may have meant that she cut the front and sides which she then curled into tendrils around her face, a style then popular.) This was for her the prime of her life, a time she would look back on with longing when she was an old woman whose body was failing but whose mind was as sharp as ever.

She and Belleria had their own horses and often rode along the banks of the Housatonic River which Hannah described as the "Sweet river of my native vale, cliff, grove and mead adorning." "In those days it was the fashion to ride double or two on a horse & a man would carry his wife to meeting on behind, and child before. However I had a horse to myself as also my cousin Belleria & side saddles of our own." Blessed with high spirits and a love of adventure, they would ride their horses for miles and miles; in fact, trips of 100 miles to Greenville, New York, to visit cousins were not uncommon. Once Hannah rode all the way to Saratoga Springs, New York, a distance of about 80 miles. Thinking back on those early times, Hannah remembered especially a warm summer day when she and Bella had ridden out through the woods to gather raspberries, only to be caught in a thunderstorm which rolled over the Housatonic River. They returned home without any raspberries, and thoroughly wet.

In a diary entry that was prompted by a beautiful fall day in her old age, but which evoked a reverie for her privileged youth, Hannah wrote:

> The wind is very high & it would seem like
> late Autumn if the trees were not so green,
> the maples south of the house are so, as are
> apple, raspberry, etc. to make quite a sum.
> [summer] appearance when the winds are

hushed; How pleasant to walk out when the
sun is mild and warm. I think the little
summer of Autumn is the most engaging
season for a contemplative mind. To loiter
in the sunny side of a hill, in view of a
small   ledge   &   rocks   sheltered   by
overhanging branches it seemed like "a holy
hermitage" was once my delight - there was
a pensive character to it, we enjoyed the
silence & beauty of the scene and the partly
color'd grove exhibiting all the hues of the
rainbow, portentous of its melancholy doom
& the shortness of its allotted time much
enhanced its value.

Being an only child meant that Hannah received special
attention from her parents of the kind normally showered
on sons. For example, her father taught her how to build
and repair clocks and watches. The intricate innards of a
timepiece spread out on a work bench, the tiny gears and
springs, the porcelain face and gold hands, were to them
both a fascination, a tiny broken cosmos to be fixed and
reordered. Appropriately, David also shared with Hannah
a love of astronomy, taking her outside on starry nights to
teach her the names of the constellations, pointing out to
her the planets which wandered among them, and teaching
her their courses throughout the year, as well as the arrival
times of comets. In a remembrance of her mother printed
as the introduction to *Mother's Poems*, Julia wrote that
David:

was also an astronomer and mathematician
and could calculate eclipses. Mother was
like him in her taste for astronomy and was
often out late at night gazing at the starry

firmament, and made herself a perpetual almanac. When it was clear she could always tell the time of night by the stars.

But more than any proficiency in any single subject or skill, Hannah seems to have received from her father a thirsty mind and a reverence for study which would last her a lifetime. He himself was a perpetual student. In November 1783 he traveled across the Housatonic River to Newtown to borrow a French Bible. The same month he "went to library took out Hopkins' Enquiry and Bellamy's Vindication." Shortly thereafter he began to keep his diary in French. Many years later, at the age of 80, Hannah wrote in her diary about the early training she received from her father and a local clergyman and remarked on her life-long love of languages:

> December 1847. 65 years ago I studied Latin a part of the time. Mr. Minor the clergyman came and heard me recite but I did not get it perfectly. My father was then dead, I had studied french under his tuition but I did not understand it as I do now for I have been reading it by turns ever since. I learned the Italian, not more than 22 or 23 years ago, but did not get that so perfectly. However, I translated Tasso and some other books which Judge Kent's brother sent me. I have not read them much lately and shall forget unless I do, but my eyesight is poor.

Hannah's knowledge as a young woman was great enough to commend her as a teacher and in 1784, just a few months prior to her 17th birthday, she traveled north to Castleton, nestled in the Green Mountains of Vermont.

Here she taught a summer school while living with an uncle. Then in August her father died suddenly of the "long [lung] fever." Giving up her job, she rode on horseback approximately 200 miles from Castleton to South Britain, covering the distance in four days. Turning to poetry as she would do so often in her life to express her feelings, she wrote:

> Here my lov'd father, here beside thy urn,
> Let fond remembrance wake the plaintive muse.
> Beneath this willow should thy orphan mourn,
> Nor the sad tribute of her tears refuse.

David was buried on top of a hillside; his grave was marked by a simple round-faced angel carved into brownstone.

As for her brief spell as a paid teacher, Hannah did not think much of it. Hannah wrote in her diary of July 11, 1849 "I gave up the schooling, the scholars were poor, chiefly. It was a rainy summer & I did not enjoy very good health while I was there which was about 3 months."

Hannah never mentioned in her diary how she came to meet the young Congregational minister, a Yale graduate by the name of Zephaniah Smith, who had taken over the pulpit of the Newtown church across the Housatonic River to the west. Of their marriage, she wrote that it took place on May 31, 1786, a clear day after a week of rain. She was eighteen years old, the groom was twenty-seven. After the wedding, she continued to live with her mother until the following December when Abigail remarried, this time to an old family friend named Eleazer Mitchel. Hannah then moved to Newtown where she and Zephaniah lived until April 1790 when Zephaniah decided he could not in good conscience continue to be a minister. Hannah was in agreement with that decision, noting years later in her diary that being the wife of a Congregational minister "is not a very desirable situation, and very few are altogether suited with it." Never again would they live in the South Britain area of Connecticut. Their destination was to the northeast and the town of Glastonbury where Zephaniah had been born and raised.

"But his delight is in the law
of Jehovah. "
Psalm 1:2

2

ZEPHANIAH HOLLISTER SMITH:

DELIGHT IN THE LAW OF JEHOVAH

Zephaniah Hollister Smith was born in the hilly section of Glastonbury known as Eastbury on August 19, 1758. The eldest son of Isaac Smith and Ruth Hollister, he was named for his maternal grandfather Zephaniah Hollister. Nothing is known of his early years except that he had two brothers and four sisters and was part of a farm family which had deep roots in Glastonbury.

In 1778, at the age of twenty he entered Yale College in New Haven, Connecticut, the only one of the sons to do so, and began to study for the ministry. The year before, Yale classes for sophomores and juniors (Spring 1777) and juniors and freshman (Fall 1777-Spring 1778) had actually been held in Glastonbury when food shortages in New

Haven and dangers of British attack from Long Island just across the Sound made holding classes in the city problematic. Although such a dispersal was a better solution than suspending classes totally, it apparently made learning difficult for the students, even though the Yale professors and tutors tried hard to maintain discipline. On November 14, Ezra Stiles, who would become president of Yale the following summer, came to observe classes. He wrote in his diary "At Glassenbury [sic] I visited Mr. Professor Strong and Mr. Tutor Baldwin...I saw the Junior Class being at Recitation with Mr. Baldwin and Made a Speech to them. Mr. Wells tells me College wants Regulations for they have left the more solid parts of Learning and run to Plays & Dramatic Exhibitions chiefly of the comic kind & turn'd College says he into Drury Lane."

Because of the difficulties of maintaining order, the Yale Corporation made the decision to have all students return to New Haven in the summer of 1778 although the threat from the British had not lessened and food shortages remained a problem. As was common practice, parents were asked to supply food so that meals could be provided at the Commons. Students were also asked to bring their own furniture for their rooms. By the time Zephaniah entered classes that fall, a sense of business-as-usual had returned to the college though life was hardly back to normal. In fact, food ran so low the next winter that vacation was extended from the standard three weeks at Christmas to seven and a half weeks, with classes resuming in the middle of February instead of early January. Then six months later in the summer of 1779, while college was still in session and Zephaniah was finishing up his freshman year, New Haven was attacked by the British.

On the 4th of July, a quiet sabbath Sunday, a British armada of 48 vessels was sighted in the Sound. Because

British ships often sailed past New Haven on route to their military headquarters in New York City, such an occurrence did not cause undo alarm until that night when the armada dropped anchor off Savin Rock at West Haven. On board were approximately 2,000 sailors and marines and about 3,000 soldiers under the command of Sir George Collier. At dawn on July 5, the day on which the town had planned a public celebration of the third anniversary of the signing of the Declaration of Independence, the troops began to come ashore. President Ezra Stiles, watching them through his telescope high in the belfry of the College Chapel, immediately decided to close the college and dismiss the students. Shortly thereafter, approximately half of the students joined with the New Haven militia headed by Captain James Hillhouse, for a total defensive force of three to four hundred men.

There is no way of knowing for certain whether Zephaniah was among the body of students that took part in the battle, but it is likely that he was for the following reasons: first, approximately one half of the Yale students took part; second, his father Isaac and his younger brother Asa had both served in the militia; and third, one of the students who led a company of over seventy students into battle was George Welles of Glastonbury, a friend of Zephaniah's.

With so few men, the efforts of the militia and students were more in the line of harassment than a full offensive. The only attack took place at West Bridge which separated West Haven from New Haven. Here the Yale students and the local militia positioned their two field pieces, then crossed the bridge to attempt to drive the British back. Elizur Goodrich, a senior who had studied in Glastonbury the previous year, recounted what happened:

I well remember the surprise we felt as we

were marching over West Bridge towards the enemy, to see Dr. Daggett [ex-President of Yale] riding furiously by us on his old black mare, with his long fowling piece in his hand, ready for action. We knew the old gentleman had studied the matter thoroughly, and settled his own mind as to the right and propriety of fighting it out, but were not quite prepared to see him come forth in so gallant a style to carry his principles into practice.

The British apparently retreated at first and the students and militia "chased after them the length of three or four fields...till we found ourselves involved with the main body, and in danger of being surrounded. It was now our turn to run, and we did for our lives."

Once they crossed the bridge, they tore it down behind them forcing the British to go further north in order to enter the city. But that only slowed them down a little. By 1:00 p.m., the Redcoats were on the green looting and pillaging at will. Although the soldiers stayed only one day, they managed to wreak much havoc in that short span of time. After they left, Stiles "visited the Desolations, dead Corpses, and Conflagrations. It was a scene of mixt Joy and Sorrow -- Plunder, Rapes, Murder, Bayoneting, Indelicacies towards the sex, Insolence and Abuse and Insult towds. the Inhab. in general, Dwellings, and Stores just setting on fire at E. Haven in full view etc.."

Fortunately, the college itself was spared and from then on to the end of the war conditions gradually improved, even though Connecticut's renegade son, Benedict Arnold, was cruising the waters of Long Island Sound like a shark, attacking suddenly and at random, hitting neighboring West Haven in August and September

1781. A particularly vicious assault was made against New London and Groton on September 5 apparently in the hopes of drawing off some of the French and American forces then pummeling Cornwallis in Virginia. Yet regardless of these strikes, there was an increasing sense of security at Yale; in fact, at the very time of these attacks, the first public commencement was held after a cessation of seven years during which period commencement was private.

It was indeed an exhilarating time to be a student at Yale. All the questions which faced the thirteen colonies struggling to win their freedom and mold themselves into a nation were debated by the students both in and out of class. In Zephaniah's senior year, during that pregnant period after the British defeat at Yorktown but before preliminary articles recognizing independence of the former colonies were signed, he and his senior classmates debated formally on whether the press ought to be free, whether there was a vacuum beyond the atmosphere, whether "the Will was determined by the greatest apparent Good" and whether "Representatives are to act their own Minds or the Minds of their Constituents." In July at the Public Examination and Presentation of Candidates for the Degree, "Sir" Smith, as he and the other seniors were addressed, took part in the traditional yearly "forensic dispute," or debate. The question which he and three other classmates had been assigned two months earlier by Ezra Stiles was "whether a representative government or a monarchy was preferable," an apt question for a new nation uncertain of how it should structure itself. Stiles did not mention in his diary how the debate turned out, but the fact that the topic was political, not religious, is indicative of what was uppermost on Stiles' mind as well as the minds of the students.

Graduation was always held in September which in 1782 was exceedingly dry, so dry in fact that the students and faculty had prayed together for divine intervention in the form of a good, hard, steady rain. Already the cattle and horses were being fed hay instead of being put out to pasture since the grass had withered and contained insufficient nutrients. Prior to receiving his diploma, Zephaniah and the other 27 seniors were tested in Greek, English, grammar, logic, geography, mathematics, philosophy, ethics, history and what Stiles called the "belles Lettres." It was a foregone conclusion that everyone was fluent in Latin since Stiles' address was delivered in that language.

Zephaniah had just turned twenty-four years old. He had the best education the colonies could give him, a respected profession, and influential classmates. In Connecticut, the door to the corridors of power was located at Yale. There were other doors but none so sure. But before Zephaniah would walk those corridors, he would enter a peculiar religious labyrinth called Sandemanianism. He would emerge thirteen years later, giving up the ministry and becoming a respected lawyer and state legislator. The labyrinth, however, would remain, being entered in turn by his daughters.

This strange turn began innocently enough. In May 1783, less than a year after graduation, Zephaniah joined the Eastbury Society (Congregational Church) along with his younger brother Asa. Then the following month on June 3, Zephaniah was licensed to preach by the Hartford Association of Ministers. For some unknown reason, nearly three years would pass before he actually headed a church, although receipts in the Historical Society of Glastonbury reveal that he may have served as interim minister in Ashford and Windham in the northeastern part of Connecticut. Ashford was without a permanent minister from the death of Reverend James Messenger in 1782 until the calling of Reverend Enoch Pond in 1789 during which time apparently several ministers preached there in hopes of being chosen to fill the vacant position. Finally on March 9, 1786 Zephaniah was called to be the minister of the Congregational Church in Newtown, Connecticut, diagonally southwest in the County of Fairfield. Though there for only four years, this period was pivotal in shaping the rest of his life and the lives of his wife and daughters.

It was here that Zephaniah became interested in the teachings of Robert Sandeman, a Scottish theologian who had come to the area in 1764 and established a small following, only to die in 1771 before solidifying the group into a structured denomination which could have influenced the Second Great Awakening. Instead, the group proved to be only a temporary thorn pricking the sides of both Congregationalism and Connecticut patriotism. Sandeman belonged to a sect called the Glasites, which had separated from the Church of Scotland under the leadership of his father-in-law, John Glas. His treatise, called *The Testimony of the King of Martyrs Concerning His Kingdom* published in 1727, caused the General Assembly in Scotland to remove Glas from the ministry, for in it he repudiated the idea of a state church. Glas then formed his own church in Dundee. Soon there were other congregations in several Scottish cities including Arbroath, Edinburgh, Perth, Dunkeld, Montrose, and Aberdeen. Glas' chief expositor was his son-in-law Robert Sandeman, who in 1757 published his *Letters on Theron and Aspasio* in response to a book by James Hervey called *Dialogues between Theron and Aspasio*. Within eleven years. Sandeman's book had reached its fourth printing and was widely read on both sides of the Atlantic. Even Samuel Langdon of Portsmouth, New Hampshire, who would become president of Harvard, saw fit to read Sandeman's work carefully and write a rebuttal called *An Impartial Examination of Mr.Robert Sandeman's Letters on Theron and Aspasio* (Boston,

1765-1769). Robert Sandeman also wrote a pamphlet published in Boston in 1764 entitled *Some Thoughts on Christianity in a Letter To a Friend By Mr. Sandeman, Author of the Letters on Theron and Aspasio To which is annexed by way of illustration The Conversion of Jonathan the Jew as Related By Himself.* To New England ministers who wallowed in theological controversy with the same grunting delight as pigs wallowing in mud, there was much in the theology of Sandeman and Glas to be stomped on and besmirched.

The central idea of John Glas and Robert Sandeman was that salvation came from the bare intellectual conviction of the truth of the gospel. Ezra Stiles hearing Sandeman preach at Newport, Rhode Island, in 1764 summed up his theology thusly:

> Which bro't him to the nature of his faith, on which he was very brief -& to this purpose, that the Iniquities of us all being laid upon Christ, he suffered for them & finished all suff'g for them on the Cross when he said it is finished & gave up the Ghost; and whosoever saw & believed this Truth that Christ finished a perfect Righteousness on the Cross, if this proposition stands true in their Mind (as he phrases it) thou shalt be saved; this and nothing but this perception is true Faith. But says he, perhaps some poor distressed Soul will say, can you give us no directions for obtaining this Light of Christ and this Faith? to which he gravely answered, no. No, says he, there are not Directions -- the simple Truth is presented to you, if you see it and believe it, it is well -- if not, you

must perish.

That being the case, Sandeman maintained that there
was no reason to have clergy or missionaries and that most
ministers were leading their flocks astray. In his *Letters on
Theron and Aspasio*, he attacked the "popular" ministers
(such as John Wesley who he considered to be "one of the
most virulent reproachers" of God ever produced in
England) because they said that acceptance by God relied
"not simply on what Christ has done, but more or less on
the use we make of him, the advance we make towards
him, or some secret desire, wish, or sigh to do so; or in
something we feel or do concerning him, by the assistance
of some kind of grace or spirit; or, lastly, on something we
employ him to do, and suppose he is yet to do for us."

In New England, where the ideas of Antinomians,
Arminians, Pelagians and Calvinists formed a strange
prickly amalgam, Sandeman's theology was vulnerable to
attack because it was unclear whether the intellectual
conviction, or as he called it the "notion" toward belief,
arose from man himself or from God. If from man, how
did the notion get there? If from God, what was the nature
of faith? (After much debate, one 19th century critic
concluded that Sandeman's entire argument was a "mere
sophism.")

Although people were interested in hearing him and
treated his ideas seriously, not many people chose to
become followers. The chief problem was not so much the
theology but the discipline which accompanied it. As
Sandeman proclaimed, "We admit none to communion with
us but those who, professing the same faith, at the same
time profess subjection to our discipline." This discipline
was rigorous, calling as it did for a full return to the
practices of the first century Christian church including
weekly "love feasts," extensive Scripture readings and

literal interpretation thereof, foot-washing, and "holy kisses." Although tolerance was not a part of the religious practices of most 18th century faiths, Sandemanianism was especially intolerant. In his *Letters on Theron and Aspasio*, Sandeman wrote:

> If anyone chooses to go to hell by a devout path, rather than by any other, let him study to form his heart on anyone of these four famous treatises: Mr. Guthrie's Trial of a Saving Interest in Christ, Mr. Marshall's Gospel Mystery of Sanctification, Mr. Boston's Human Nature in its Fourfold State, and Dr. Doddridge's Rise and Progress of Religion in the Soul. If any profane person, who desires to be converted, shall take pains to enter into the spirit of these books it will be easy to show from the New Testament that he thereby becomes twofold more the child of hell than he was before.

But besides the theology and the all-or-nothing quality of membership, one particular discipline presented an almost insurmountable barrier to membership. Sandeman preached that followers must not lay up treasures on Earth, for Christ had said in Matthew 6:19-21 "Lay not up for yourselves treasures upon earth, where moth and rust doth corrupt, and where thieves break through and steal: But lay up for yourselves treasures in heaven, where neither moth nor rust doth corrupt, and where thieves do not break through nor steal. For where your treasure is, there will your heart be also." Living by faith in God alone without saving anything for the morrow but giving it instead to charity may have been morally compelling, but the inherent thriftiness and pragmatism of both the Scots and the New Englanders made it virtually impossible for the majority to achieve.

Another problem in terms of attracting followers on this side of the Atlantic was that a strict interpretation of the New Testament also led to acceptance and support of whatever government was in power, based on the fact that both Jesus and Paul called for Christians to be law-abiding citizens who did not foment rebellion, no matter how grievous the wrongs, because rulers were appointed by God. This meant loyalty to the monarchy, but Sandeman arrived in the colonies in 1764, a time when dissatisfaction with the king was mounting rapidly.

Regardless of these problems, there were many ministers in the colonies who found the thinking of John Glas and Robert Sandeman compelling in part because Congregationalism was for all intents and purposes a state church, a concept Glas had repudiated and which was causing problems in the colonies due to the increase in other forms of Protestantism, including the Church of England and Baptist. Furthermore, Sandeman questioned the role of ministers at a time when many ministers were themselves questioning their roles. Rapid growth and increased diversity in towns and cities had resulted in a steady erosion of clerical power and influence. If, as Sandeman maintained, salvation relied entirely on the grace of God made possible by the sacrifice of Jesus, then ministers were superfluous.

Although a cursory review of eighteenth century theology may indicate that it was a seamless, serene whole, in fact the churches in the colonies were riven with dissent, much of which turned on the nature of faith versus works and whether God was known more correctly and completely through the emotions or through the intellect. The memory was still strong of the Great Awakening, a period of intense religious revival throughout New England and the Middle Atlantic states and to a lesser degree in the South in the 1730s and 1740s. People were still seeking answers to the questions it raised as to the significance of personal religious experience. In contrast to the endless, arcane debates between the New Lights (who generally viewed the Great Awakening as a positive occurrence) and the Old Lights (who viewed it as a woeful aberration), there was an astringent cleansing quality in the thinking of John Glas and Robert Sandeman. According to them, man could not take any credit for coming to know God whether through the intellect or the emotions, therefore the argument between New Lights and Old Lights was moot.

As will be seen, it is exactly this point which led Julia Smith in the middle of the next century to translate the Bible from Hebrew, Greek, and Latin in a stilted literal way, believing that knowledge of God would come not from a person reading the words but from God himself imparting meaning through the spirit. Quoting from Paul (II Corinthians 3:6), she said in her introduction to the Bible that "the letter kills but the spirit gives life," by which she meant that though the impulse to know God might arise in the human soul, the knowledge itself is God-given and is not reliant on human endeavor even though human endeavor is a necessary precursor.

There is no way to know how Zephaniah felt about the nature of God at the time he entered the ministry, but at least two factors indicate he was probably an "Old Light" Congregationalist: first, he grew up under the tutelage of Rev. James Eells, the Old Light minister of the Eastbury Congregational Church; second, he was at Yale under the presidency of Ezra Stiles, an Old Light with an Enlightenment afterglow. Mistrustful of the excessive emotionalism of some New Light thinkers, Stiles stressed instead a worldly intellectualism. Besides encouraging political debate on campus, as evidenced by "Sir" Smith's graduation topic, Stiles imparted to his students the idea that the United States deserved to take its place on a global stage both politically and intellectually. In short, he was a man who valued highly the pursuit of knowledge congruent to the pursuit of the knowledge of God. Dynamic and energetic, he left his mark on every Yale student under his tutelage which would have included Zephaniah. At the same time, Sandemanianism (as the Glasites were called in the colonies) was not unknown at Yale and in fact two tutors (a position the equivalent of assistant professor) had been expelled from Yale in 1765 by President Thomas Clap for professing support for Sandeman. There was also a small congregation of Sandemanians in New Haven, so it is not unlikely that Zephaniah had heard of the group while he was a student.

The church in Newtown to which Zephaniah would be called as minister in 1786 had been headed until 1776 by Rev. David Judson, a man who had read *Letters on Theron and Aspasio*, and was sufficiently impressed by them to write to Sandeman himself. His letters, as well as those from other clergy in the area including Rev. Ebenezer White of Danbury, encouraged Sandeman to leave Scotland in August 1764 and travel to New England as a missionary where he visited several cities including Boston, Portland, Maine, and Newport, Rhode Island. But although he had some success in these cities, the group which was most sympathetic to his theology was located in Fairfield County and lower Litchfield County in the southwest corner of Connecticut. In fact, in May 1763, the year before Sandeman even came to the colonies, Rev. Ebenezer White of the Danbury Church and Rev. James Taylor of the New Fairfield South Church had been "held to trial and silenced" on account of "false doctrine" by a council of the local Congregational Consociation. The following March, the council found White's sympathies toward Sandeman's theology to be so strong that they dismissed him from his Danbury pastorate. But White, who had been minister of the Danbury Church for 28 years, and a majority of his congregation refused to accept that order; instead, they formed the New Danbury Church which openly accepted Sandemanianism, although it did not immediately adopt all the disciplines that Sandeman required.

With such support, it was natural that in 1766 Robert Sandeman made Danbury his headquarters, but his work was hindered both by hostility from many clergymen (as evidenced by the censure of Rev. White by the Fairfield East Consociation) and his insistence on loyalty to the crown. Then in 1771 at the age of 53 he died of unknown causes at the Danbury home of a loyal disciple named Theophilus Chamberlain. Still, his theology continued to spread, albeit slowly. In 1772 a group from the Danbury congregation moved to New Haven where a new church was formed which included some Yale graduates. Meanwhile the Danbury church became stronger under the leadership of Rev. White's son. But the Revolutionary War made life extremely difficult for Sandemanians; in fact, several sold their property and fled to Canada to avoid persecution as Tories. This more than any other factor spelled doom for the sect. Although Sandemanianism remained influential in the Fairfield area for several years following the Revolutionary War, its power waned until by the 1830s there was only one small congregation left in Danbury.

As had the Danbury Church under Rev. Ebenezer White, the Newtown Church ran into rough water well before the Revolutionary War due to its support of Sandeman. But unlike the Danbury Church which was summarily thrown out of the local ecclesiastical boards, the Newtown Church under Rev. Judson decided to withdraw voluntarily "on account of dissatisfaction with principles of discipline contained in the Platform," which is a reference to the Saybrook Platform. On March 22, 1774, the Consociation met and ruled as follows "Mr. Judson & this church were dismissed from this Consociation but not from the communion of the churches." Rev. Judson died on September 24, 1776, and the pulpit remained vacant for ten years until Zephaniah was ordained pastor in 1786. What this indicates is that the Newtown Church was already identifying itself as Sandemanian at the time that Zephaniah accepted the call. Only speculation is possible as to why he would have gone to such a renegade congregation. One ecclesiastical history states that he "was ordained pastor by a select Council in 1786," which may mean that he was sent to the church by an outside governing body, but this would have been highly unusual given the local autonomy of the Congregational churches. Furthermore, there is no mention of such a council in the records of the Fairfield East Consociation and the Fairfield East Association. Another possibility is that he was already familiar with Sandemanianism, having come in contact with it while in New Haven. The third possibility is that he thought he could bring the church back into the orthodox theological fold, although if this were true, he would probably have rejoined the Consociation and Association, which neither he nor his church did. Even if it were true that he came with the intent of correcting the church's doctrinal errors, the opposite was to occur. As reported in the *Sketch of the Fairfield East Association*, Zephaniah:

> subsequently embraced much of the sentiments of the sect of the Glassites, or Sandemanians, and painful divisions arose in the church. He was dismissed by the society in 1790. A small Sandemanian church was

formed, to which he preached for a few months, when he left the ministry, and afterwards removed to Glastenbury, and became a lawyer....The church was so much scattered and enfeebled by these distractions, which continued for several years, that it was formally reorganized, Sept. 26, 1799, with only nine members. The next pastor, Jehu Clark, was ordained Oct. 23, 1799, and then the church came back into the Consociation.

Although it is unclear whether he came to adopt all the practices of Sandemanianism, such as the washing of feet, Zephaniah was strongly affected by its doctrine. Ezra Stiles wrote in his diary on February 26, 1789:

Revd Mr. Smith of Newtown in Connect. has been reformg & new modellg his CHH, and after several Manouvres of Discipline & omission of the Sacrmt of the Lds Supper (so that it has been administered but once in a Twelvemonth) he lately administered it to those who assented to his Reform, & in the Administra publickly refused to deliver the sacramental Elements to Seventeen Members of his Chh. in full Communion & under no Censure.

One idea which made Zephaniah especially uneasy was that ministers should not accept money for their services. According to Julia, Zephaniah's daughter:

My father visited the Rev. Mr. Wildman, a noted Congregational clergyman of South

Britain, to talk over the subject. Mr.
Wildman believed just as he did in regard to
preaching for money, and he advised my
father to quit preaching at once, as he was a
young man; and he added, "I would do so if
I were younger, but I am too old to dig, and
to beg I am ashamed." My father went
home and made preparations to abandon the
ministry.

Zephaniah followed his advice and left the ministry in
1790, apparently leaving the church in Newtown in
disarray. According to one source, "he finally abandoned
his charge without being dismissed, leaving the church
almost a wreck, floating upon the troubled sea without a
pilot and almost without a crew."

The decision must have been an exceedingly difficult
and painful one for Zephaniah. Giving up the ministry was
a very grave step in a society where local ministers served
in the multiple roles of spiritual, political, and educational
leaders. Apart from how his peers would view such a
defection, Zephaniah also had to struggle with how God
would view it, for it is clear that his faith was deep and
abiding. In one of only three extant sermons from this
period, Zephaniah wrote:

May we continue to contemplate much upon
the dying love of our dear Lord that hereby
we may be constrained to love him with all
our hearts to devote ourselves entirely to his
service and to live lives of an eternal holy
obedience to his commands so that when he
shall be revealed from heaven with his holy
angels in flaming fire -- taking vengeance on
them that know not God and that obey not

the Gospel we may be found of him in
peace, clothed with the robes of his
righteousness and receive from that glorious
welcome - Come ye blessed of my father
inherit the kingdom purchased for you from
the land of the world.

Although Zephaniah did not continue to be a
Sandemanian, it is clear that he, his wife, and eventually
his daughters would remain theologically sympathetic to the
sect throughout their lives. As will be seen, Julia separated
permanently from the Congregational Church in the 1820s
and actually called herself a Sandemanian. Her later
assertion that the "letter kills but the spirit gives life," i.e.
that human understanding is a gift from God and cannot be
achieved by human endeavor, is similar to Sandeman's
assertion of the "bare work of Jesus Christ." Nothing man
did, no righteousness of any kind, no study of any amount,
could win for man God's acceptance.

When Zephaniah returned to Glastonbury, it is likely
that he was seen as a bit of a rebel or at the very least a
free-thinker. In fact, the label "Sandemanian" seemed to
stick to Zephaniah his entire life, even though he and his
family attended the First Congregational Church in
Glastonbury and his funeral at the age of 77 was conducted
by the Congregational minister. It would also stick to Julia
so that her Bible translation would occasionally be
identified as Sandemanian.

For a short while after leaving the ministry, Zephaniah
worked as a merchant before deciding to become a lawyer,
a profession which was entered by studying under another
lawyer, an educational practice called reading law. The
man under whose tutelage Zephaniah chose to read law was
Jonathan Brace, a respected lawyer who represented
Glastonbury in the Connecticut General Assembly. This

was a propitious decision for, as will be seen, the Smiths bought Brace's home and farm when he and his family decided to move to Hartford. The land along the Connecticut River was among the most fertile and most valued in the entire state. It was far better than the land in Eastbury on which Zephaniah had spent his childhood; its purchase helped ensure prosperity for the Smiths. Of equal importance, Jonathan Brace would go on to become one of the most influential men in the state during the first two decades of the nineteenth century. He was a member of the Council of the General Assembly from 1802 to 1818, a position of considerable power. He was also a judge of the county court, judge of the probate court, state's attorney for Hartford, and mayor of Hartford, to name only some of his positions. In short, in a Federalist world where friendship counted for a great deal, Zephaniah had a powerful ally in Jonathan Brace.

After completing his studies, Zephaniah joined the bar in 1796 and practiced law until 1833 when he was 74 years old. A staunch Federalist, he represented the Town of Glastonbury in nine sessions of the State Legislature. According to town records, he also took his turn at local government jobs. At a town meeting in 1794 he was appointed along with Major John Hale to "get ferry between Glastonbury and Rocky Hill granted to Glastonbury." In 1796 he served as a "fence viewer," a job which entailed walking property lines to make certain boundary markers were maintained. In 1798 he was appointed lawyer for the town. In 1801 he was moderator for the annual town meeting. At other times he audited the town treasurer's accounts and served on the Board of Relief.

For six years from 1798 until 1803, Zephaniah also served as Justice of the Peace for Hartford County, an appointment made by the State Legislature. According to

Richard Purcell in his book *Connecticut in Transition, 1775-1818*, justices of the peace "were annually appointed by the Legislature and hence, like the sheriff, represented the state in the locality. As such, they advised in the executive affairs of the community. The senior justice had charge of the local elections. With the selectmen and constables, they named the tavern keepers; bound men to keep the peace; and apprehended suspects. Their jurisdiction was confined within the town, but their warrants only by the state. Their jurisdiction was not unlike that of the English justice of the peace."

Obviously, Zephaniah's Sandemanian proclivities did not hinder him from becoming an influential man in Glastonbury. But of greatest importance was the influence he had on his five daughters. Julia often noted in her diary that her father was performing a wedding in his office, or was traveling on legal business to neighboring towns, or staying in Hartford overnight because court was in session. She also studied the law text she always referred to simply as "Blackstone" and apparently, after her father's death, would on occasion help friends and neighbors with legal problems.

It is highly doubtful that the Smiths would have become deeply involved in abolition and suffrage had Zephaniah stayed a Congregational minister instead of choosing to become a lawyer. As much as his Sandemanian ideas, his career helped shape the way his entire family viewed the world.

*"Which will give its fruit
in its time."*
Psalm 1:3

3

THE EARLY YEARS IN GLASTONBURY

Only after Zephaniah's theological change of heart was the decision made to sell the Hickok homestead in South Britain and move to Glastonbury. Julia Smith related the following story to a relative about that sale:

> When Mother sold the farm in South Britain she told the man who came to bargain for it that he could have it for 600 pounds. He said he would give L595, but she would not let him have it for that and he drove off. My Father said, "Now you have lost a chance to sell the farm." She replied, "A man would not come fifty miles to buy a farm and give it up for L5." And she was right. The man

drove a mile or two and then turned back
and bought the farm for 600 pounds. That
sum paid for two thirds of the place and my
father paid the rest.

After a brief period in the Eastbury section of
Glastonbury (where he had been born and raised), during
which Zephaniah worked as a merchant, and a six-month
period in Windham, Connecticut, (May to October 1794),
during which Zephaniah represented Windham at the state
legislature, the Smiths finally achieved stability. In 1795
the growing family purchased the farm and the large house
on Main Street from Anna Kimberly Brace and her
husband Judge Jonathan Brace, under whose tutelage
Zephaniah had studied law. After nine years of upheaval
which included three professions -- minister, merchant, and
lawyer -- and at least six moves, Zephaniah and Hannah
settled down to raise their daughters. Four had been born
already and each had been given an evocative name: the
eldest was named Hancy Zephina (1787), probably a
derivation of Hannah and Zephaniah (in later life this
daughter wrote her name H. Zephina); the second was
named Cyrinthia Sacretia (1788) which bespeaks her
parent's love of Latin and Greek classics; the third was
named poetically Laurilla Aleroyla (1789), and the fourth
was named Julietta Abelinda (1792) at birth, but Zephaniah
changed her name shortly thereafter to Julia Evelina after
the popular novel *Evelina, or A Young Lady's Entrance
Into The World* by Fanny Burney, in which the young
heroine rises from humble origins to social prominence.
Only the last child, born in 1797, was given an "ordinary"
name of Biblical derivation -- Abby Hadassah was named
for her grandmother Abigail and her mother Hannah
Hadassah, and as a child she was called Abba. Julia
recalled years later "We used to have a saying that three of

us were the daughters of a clergyman, one the daughter of a merchant and one of a lawyer."

The Smith house was located on a very narrow piece of land, 22 1/2 rods wide (approximately 371 feet) which stretched for three miles from the Connecticut River through the fertile meadow lands and finally to the wooded hills. Such a long thin lot was normal for the riverfront town of Glastonbury for it gave to landowners rights not only to the river but to various terrains needed to make a living on a farm. Only seven miles from Hartford, the Smith land was ideally located for a farming family with a cosmopolitan mindset. Not only did they travel to Hartford to market their crops but also to buy books, attend French club meetings, try court cases, and visit friends. On April 26, 1798 Hannah wrote to her mother:

> ...we are very busy in preparing for the election having five girls to be fix [sic] out and some of them old enough to think their clothes must be made in the very newest fashion and their bonnets made in Hartford so we have been obliged to get them, besides I am going this election to Hartford as Mr. Smith is to go to the Assembly. Mrs. Cogswell says her sister Amaretta will be there and she wishes me to come -- I have wean'd my baby and Mrs. Conly will take care of her.

Although they moved easily in both an urban and rural environment, it was the farm which took up the majority of their time. On it they raised a wide variety of crops and livestock. Right up to her death at age 83, Hannah was deeply involved in the farm's management. At age 81, she wrote in her diary, April 25, 1849, "It is clear and pleasant, somewhat cool - p.m. It has been so pleasant I have worked at the old grapevine with Glazier all the forenoon." Her diary and the diary of her daughter Julia are filled with notations about taking onions to market, selling peaches, harvesting peas, the birth and death of farm animals, and the hiring of help to harvest the crops, slaughter livestock, and cut firewood for the winter. Hannah Smith's account book for the years 1821-24, as analyzed by Nancy Cott in her book *The Bonds of Womanhood: "Woman's Sphere" in New England, 1780-1835*, is illuminating:

> She recorded the purchase of edibles and baking supplies (spices, plums, currants, raisins, sugar, molasses, salt, wine, coffee, tea); of household items (teacups, platters, chest, jug, box, coffeepot, tinware, pins) and construction materials (pine boards, nails, steel); of writing accoutrements (paper, penknife, spelling book), nursing supplies (camphor, plaister) and soap, and some luxuries (snuff, tobacco, shell combs, parasol). Furthermore, she purchased at least eleven different kinds of cloth (such as dimity, brown holland, "factory cloth"), four kinds of yarn and thread, leather, and buttons; bought silk shawls, bonnets, dresses, stockings, and kid gloves, and also paid for people's services in making clothing. The farm produced the marketable commodities of grain (oats, rye, corn) and timber, animals (calves, turkeys, fowl) and animal products (eggs, hens' feathers, quills, wool, pork), and other farm produce which required more human labor, such as butter,

cider, lard, and tallow.

Their lifestyle could best be described as genteel agrarian. Sometimes there was live-in hired help. On September 16, 1799, Hannah wrote to her mother "The negro wench lived with me about eight months so I have had help the chief of the time." More often they hired people to help with specific jobs such as wood-cutting, harvesting crops, or preserving foods. The only thing that set them apart was that Zephaniah's law career gave the family a financial advantage over people who derived their entire living from farming. Zephaniah often traveled to try cases or to attend the legislature in Hartford, yet he was also involved with running the farm with his wife, daughters and, for a twelve-year period, his mother-in-law. Abigail Hickok Mitchel came to live with the Smiths following the death of her second husband. She lived with them for 12 years until her death in 1831 at the age of 92. This meant there were seven strong-minded women in the household during that period and one equally strong-minded man. Fortunately, Zephaniah had a sense of humor as shown by a plea written to the Smith women in legal language:

> To the sheriff of the county of the kitchen or her deputy or other of the constables of the Town of Buttery Cupboard within said county -- greetings. By authority of the housekeeper you are hereby commanded to summon the Pancake Bowl together with the frying pan both of said cupboard trading in company under the firm of frying cake to appear before the fire in the kitchen...to answer unto several stomachs.

Hannah jested right back at him in verse. She had been trying to get Zephaniah to fix the garden fence, a job that he had apparently put off one too many times. Not one to ask directly again, she wrote him the following tongue-in-cheek poem (excerpted):

But first of all, the garden wall,
   Tis requisite to mention,
As we conjecture, its architecture
   Is quite a new invention.

Part is so high, 'twould brave the sky,
   Had not old Boreas shattered,
And rueful battle with the cattle,
   Unfortunately battered.

One place is pales, another rails,
   But boards compose the front, all;
Some in particular, rise perpendicular
   And some lie horizontal.

Next the inside, which forms the pride
   Of curious cultivators
Where roses grow, and tulips blow
   Mid onions and potatoes...

A row of peas, a flock of geese,
   A piece of flax and clover -
A patch of oats, a dozen shoats
   That range the garden over.

No matter how busy she was with running the farm, raising the children, and trying to get Zephaniah to fix garden fences, Hannah always found the chance to read and translate, two of her primary intellectual interests. Between shelling peas and tucking the youngest into bed, cooking pumpkin pies and chasing cows who had wandered into the corn, there were pockets of time when French could be translated, the works of a Latin poet could be studied, and Italian could be learned. Several small, hand-bound folios of her translations and studies are owned by the Historical Society of Glastonbury; among them are lists of the Bishops of Rome, lists of the kings of Scotland and Portugal, lists of Greco-Egyptian Ptolemies, and classical love letters translated from Italian.

Besides writing in small folios, she also wrote on the backs of envelopes, along the edges of advertisements, and in the margins of letters sent to her. White space was a prized possession to be filled with snippits of poems and drafts of petitions. Other than the difficulty of getting sufficient paper as well as quill pens which wrote clearly (a constant source of irritation to her), Hannah's chief difficulty was getting the books to translate. In 1825 she was delighted to receive seven volumes of Italian from an unknown benefactor. In a letter dated September 1825 with only the salutation of "Sir," Hannah wrote:

> I have lately received a very valuable present from the liberality of a person unknown to me. Ariosto's Orlando Furioso, Tasso's Aminta & Pignotti's Fables. These works of the most famous Italian poets I prize very highly indeed. They arrived so opportunely just as I was thinking I must relinquish the study of this pleasuring language for want of books, that they are a real treasure. They have afforded me much amusement. I am still occupied and quite diverted with Orlando Furioso. There are in this work so many different scenes and

characters so many chieftains, armies, feats of chivalry and curious enchantments that one is continually surprised & pleased with the masterly invention of the author. I have been more entertained as I knew nothing of the contents having only heard that it was written by Ariosto. I am likewise pleased with the other books. I cannot express how much I feel indebted to the donor of these seven volumes. Should he come to Connecticut again, I should hope to have the satisfaction of making my acknowledgment personally.

Long after Hannah's death when the taxation battle was raging, *The Hartford Courant* reported the following anecdote told them by Julia relating to the gift of the books. Julia said that she "was riding in a stage to Sackett's Harbor; that Judge Kent of Jefferson County, brother of Chancellor Kent, was also a passenger, and that he, out of regard for her knowledge of the French language (of which she had been a teacher in the Troy seminary), and having learned that her mother understood the Italian, presented to her, for her mother, some beautifully bound Italian volumes." This is supported by Hannah's diary entry of December 1847 in which she mentions books sent to her by Judge Kent's brother.

Hannah's translations are intriguing because she often combined her skills as a poet and linguist by translating poetry, even attempting to put ancient Greek writing into meter and rhyme. The following segment from Sappho is illustrative:

As poets say, the gods benighted
At a cottage door once alighted.

And after eating, drinking, sleeping
To pay the peasant for their keeping,
Bade him ask what most he wanted,
And it should be fully granted.
He asked a son without woman,
A wish defined before by no man.
The gods bestowed it on him knowing
To what this odd request was owing.

Such deep interest in languages and translation was not unusual for an early nineteenth-century "woman of letters." In her book *Perish the Thought: Intellectual Women in Romantic America, 1830-1860,* Susan Conrad explained that translation was a culturally acceptable role for women because it did not clash with the tenets of "true womanhood" and it kept them aloof from the controversial reform stances of feminist thinkers:

Because of the "appropriateness" of her work and the attention commanded by occasional popular successes, the "woman of Letters" was most instrumental in enlarging the intellectual territory of American women. At the same time, she was often most discontented with the role she had elaborated. She was too intellectually adventurous to abide by any procedures implicit in history, translation, and literary criticism that meshed nicely with the tenets of ideal femininity.

An apt description of Hannah, it works equally well for all five daughters. As will be seen, they all chafed at cultural restrictions although they protested with propriety, even humor. For example, during their notorious tax battle with the Town of Glastonbury in the 1870s, Julia and Abby named their last two unconfiscated cows Taxey and Votey, and declared them to be two creatures who naturally should go together.

Translation was only one of Hannah's myriad abilities. As has been seen, she was an accomplished poet who wrote mainly for herself and her family, although some of her poems were printed in local newspapers and magazines. She was a clockmaker who enjoyed tinkering with mechanical objects, a skill she had learned from her father. She was a beekeeper who filled her diary with notes on Chatham hives, bees swarming, and selling honey. She also maintained her interest in astronomy. In one poem titled "The Comet of 1823," Hannah wrote of the constellations "north of the Ecliptic" which she marked by an asterisk. She used a dagger to mark stars belonging to those constellations mentioned immediately before them. Here is an excerpt:

> Little stranger wandering high,
>   Is it now thy festal year
> With the gentry of the sky,
>   In the northern hemisphere?
> Heroes thron'd with king and queen,
>   Crown'd with sparkling diadems,
> Princes, demigods, are seen
>   There adorned with blazing gems --
> Welcom'd by the starry host,
>   Hercules* kneeling will receive thee,
> And the hundred orbs he boasts,
>   A resplendent chaplet, weave thee.
>
> Art thou pleas'd with beauty's charms?
>   There's many an eye its lustre beaming,
> If chivalry thy bosom warms,

Many a knight in armor gleaming.
Auriga* with his helmet on,
   In Capella's+ radiance glowing --
Bootes* known in ages gone,
   His fame to bright Arcturus+ owing,
And Ophiacus* thou wilt view,
   Chief of an ancient wily crew...

Dost thou relish huntsman glee?
   All the chase affords is there,
Royal game of high degree,
   Lion,* Unicorn and Bear.
Flight, pursuit, and merry sport,
   Pastime of the polar court;
Greyhounds* fleet in full career,
Charles'* Heart is throbbing near,
Ursa Major in the track,
Dubhe,+ Alioth,+ Benetnack...

All created forms and more
   Than earth, air, or ocean bred
Monsters, so renown'd of yore,
   Fish, and fowl, and quadruped,
Thou wilt see, at present polish'd,
Their old habits all abolish'd.
   Cerberus* once a wizard grim,
Now a glittering dandy for us
   Since he left the regions dim --
And Pouiatowsky's modern Taurus
Courteous groups of Serpents* twining
   The old Dragon in his den,
With his visage smooth and shining,
   In the beams of Rastaben.+

Even as an old woman, she attempted to maintain the astronomical knowledge she had worked so hard to acquire earlier in life. Just before her seventy-eighth birthday, she wrote in her diary on July 21, 1854 "...warm, clear and windy. Risley reaping, Abby mowing. I have been trying to remember a little Astronomy. Mercury goes on its orbit 109 thousand miles an hour, Venus 80, the earth 68 & Mars 55, Jupiter 30, Tatur 22 [unclear] 1000 miles an hour, Juno 1000, Vista 1000."

Although not reclusive, Hannah valued highly her privacy and quiet, values she passed on to her daughters. She noted in her diary of December 5, 1847 "64 years ago I wrote in the evening not having any inclination to spend any time with Company, I had thought fit to betake myself to my study and I have tho't very much so ever since, rather being in my study than any where." This withdrawn studiousness is important in regard to the nature of the Smiths' abolition and suffrage activities. Neither the mother nor the daughters were at ease in the public arena, with Abby being the only possible exception; as an elderly woman she became the family spokesperson on the issue of taxation without representation. It must also be pointed out, however, that even had they chosen to enter the public arena, it would have been difficult because they were women, a point which will be discussed later.

The Smiths were extremely fortunate to have no deaths in the family caused by childhood diseases such as scarlet fever or whooping cough. When illness did occur, Hannah and Zephaniah worked together to combat it. In February 1812 when Julia was nineteen, she was very ill for several weeks. Zephina wrote to her grandmother Abigail Mitchel that "Papa nor Mama have not had their clothes off since she was sick though Mama does not seem as overcome with fatigue as Papa. We take turns in watching with her. I am sitting by the side of her and Mama is rocking her for we have [had] rockers put on the bedstead and Papa is up chamber asleep."

The daughters' relationship with their father seems always to have been very good. Zephaniah was happy to indulge their thirst for books but apparently stirred up Julia's ire on a few occasions when he failed to return from Hartford with the desired text. In one story written down after Julia's death, it is said that when she was fourteen she wanted her father to bring home a Latin grammar. When he returned without it, she rode to Hartford on horseback before breakfast to get it herself. In another story, the boys plagued her and said a girl studying Latin must be going to college, but the more they plagued, the more she persisted. Whether this story is true or not, it is at least in character. She often noted in her diary that her father had brought her books. For example, on December 24, 1814, Zephaniah traveled to Hartford with his father-in-law Eleazer Mitchel who was visiting from South Britain. "In the morning Father went to Hartford with Grandfather before I got up. I knitted. Electa Kellogg came over in the afternoon and stayed about an hour. Father bought three new books -- The American Orator and the Campaign in Russia, two volumes." Another entry on February 20, 1816 records "Fine weather this evening. Father went to Hartford. I read French. Knitted. Father returned this evening and bought me a Greek Grammar. The price was seven shillings and six pence."

Julia followed his legal career with some interest and often noted in her diary when and where he was arguing court cases. Sometimes local cases were tried at the Smith house whereas Julia received first-hand exposure to the legal system, an exposure which would prove useful during her tax battle with Glastonbury half a century later. Being Justice of the Peace, Zephaniah also performed marriages in his office which was attached to the house.

It would be a mistake to assume that because the Smiths were spending so much time reading and thinking that they were removed from the world socially. Although by the 1830s, the family had closed around itself to a degree, up through the 1820s the Smiths led a very active social life. As an octogenarian deeply involved in woman's suffrage, Julia remembered her childhood selectively, at one point saying she had been required to go to dances, but her own diary gives the lie to that statement. She loved dances. In 1811 she went to a ball at the Hale household at which there were 34 ladies and 22 gentlemen. "I danced almost every time. We came home at 3 o'clock. We had a very fine dance. Mr. Simons spent the rest of the night here." At the age of 23 while visiting her grandparents in South Britain, she was invited to a dance in Woodbury. The day before, she sewed on her lace and embroidered dress, trying to finish it in time. The next day, she wrote:

> I finished my dress and washed and ironed it with my other things...At seven I dressed for the dance and a little later J. Mitchel came over with Sarah Osborn and I went in the carriage with them to Woodbury to the ball. I danced thirteen or fourteen times...The ball was over at two.

Young men often came calling and some clearly perceived themselves as suitors. On February 2, 1812 when she was sick, just before her diary breaks off for six weeks, she wrote that "Mr. Strong sent me a note, inviting me to go with him to a ball that will be next Wednesday, But I will not go."

Besides dances, Julia wrote about playing Blind Man's Bluff with her sisters, singing songs, practicing the piano, playing chess with her mother, gathering nuts in the meadows, admiring Laurilla's paintings (of which the entire family was very proud), and constantly visiting and being visited by friends. On a day which sums up the Smiths during the second decade, Julia wrote on November 14, 1815:

> Did my ironing, sewed on my petticoat.
> Zephina and Cyrinthia went to Hartford to
> see Mrs. Norton. Laurilla is painting a
> picture in the best chamber. Abby is in the
> kitchen and I myself am alone in the living
> room today. It is very cold. I knitted a little
> on my glove, read in the French newspaper,
> the law and the B. [Bible]. Zephina and
> Cyrinthia returned at six. I knitted this
> evening on my cotton stocking.

The other main activity in their lives, which would continue until they died, was charity work in the town. Julia often mentioned going to visit sick people or making clothes for the poor. Her entry on May 22, 1818 is typical. "Made the breakfast, etc. Cloudy. I made some butter. Zephina and I went this afternoon in the carriage to see Alice Lindsay who has been sick and we took her some provisions. We went to see Mrs. Wickham who has just lost her child. She was grief stricken." So great were the Smiths' charitable activities that when the last two sisters refused to pay property taxes, many men in town were slow to criticize them because of the good works they had done for so many people.

It was charitable activity which brought them into close contact with the few families of African descent in Glastonbury. While recognizing their need, the Smiths also came to recognize the injustice that helped create that need. So too, the effects of an alcoholic husband and father on his wife and children were made clear to the Smiths via their charitable work, leading them to support the temperance movement. Though ladies of charity were very common, ladies of charity who paused and evaluated the reasons why the charity was needed in the first place and then attempted to do away with the underlying injustice were rare indeed.

*"And all which he shall do
shall be prospered."
Psalm 1:3b*

4

SISTERHOOD/ SPINSTERHOOD

Because of their own intellectual bent, Hannah and Zephaniah considered a good education of great importance for their daughters. However, their idea of a good education varied in significant ways from the idea of most of their contemporaries. Education for women during this period focused on increasing their social usefulness as wives and mothers; anything beyond the most rudimentary reading and ciphering, a little music and needlework was seen as not only unnecessary but dangerous for it would rob them of their charms and make them restive and "uppity." According to a much quoted anonymous work of the period entitled *Sketches of the History, Genius and Disposition of the Fair Sex* published in 1812, women were "born for a life of uniformity and dependence." Therefore, genius would only "make them regret the station which Providence has assigned them, or have recourse to unjustifiable ways to get from it. The best taste for science only contributes to make them particular. It takes them away from the simplicity of their domestic duties, and from general society, of which they are the loveliest ornament..."

Hannah and Zephaniah rejected this approach to educating women. To them, the best education for their daughters was identical to what they would have offered sons, which meant heavy emphasis on the classics, history, mathematics, and languages. In a letter sent to her mother, Abigail Hickok Mitchel, dated August 2, 1800, Hannah wrote that thirteen-year-old Zephina, the oldest daughter, had been sent to attend a boarding school in Norwich, Connecticut, which Hannah considered better than the one in Litchfield, a reference to the school run by Sarah Pierce. The school in Norwich was a boys' academy which admitted girls. Later on the girls apparently did attend Litchfield Academy as evidenced by letters that passed back and forth between Hannah and her daughters. While Sarah Pierce wanted every girl to "show a sweet temper, a modest deportment on all occasions," she also warned that "there is no moment when the mind is stationary, if not moving onward its orbit is retrograde," an idea with which the Smiths would have been in complete agreement. Courses which were offered at her school included geography, composition, grammar, arithmetic, history, moral and natural philosophy, Biblical history, logic, English literature, botany, mineralogy, chemistry, piano, music, and drawing. For $5.00 extra, students could also take French lessons.

The Smith girls also studied in Glastonbury whenever a suitable tutor was available. When Abby was 12 years old, she wrote the following letter to her grandmother:

> May 23, 1809 Dear Grandmother...I went to
> school last winter to Mr. Wright and studied
> geography & arithmetic and I have braided
> me a new straw bonnet and intend to help
> spin the carpet but it takes me most all my
> time to run after the geese, fetch the cows
> and help puppie drive the sheep and I have
> to do all the errands because I am the
> youngest.

When they had surpassed the resources available in these schools, the Smiths were innovative in finding new avenues for education. For example, both Julia and Abby spent at least one summer each living with a French family named Value in New Haven to improve their proficiency in the language. Refugees from Haiti, the Values took in students as boarders. They also taught dancing and hosted meetings of French clubs. Long after her summer with them, Julia wrote to them in French and visited a branch of the family in Hartford. She also endeavored to maintain proficiency in the language by keeping her diary from age 18 to age 50 in French (which may explain why her entries are short and matter-of-fact).

The older sisters also took responsibility for teaching the younger sisters. For example, throughout 1813 when Abby was 16 years old and Julia was 21 years old, Julia tutored Abby in Latin. Every day Abby recited to her from Virgil, Cicero and other Roman authors, a task Abby apparently found onerous at times. Julia also taught Abby by example: in 1816 she decided to teach herself Greek, using the Greek grammar which her father had brought her from Hartford. She began to study three to four hours a day, exhibiting the concentration she would show several years later when she translated the Bible from Hebrew, Greek and Latin five times, attempting each time to get closer to the original meaning.

The family's tie to Yale College, from which Zephaniah had graduated, was very strong as evidenced by the fact that at least some members traveled to New Haven every September for many years to attend commencement, which they considered an important social and intellectual occasion. There were dances, dinners, speeches, sermons, and much visiting with friends. It was, in fact, the social highlight of the year for the Smiths during the first two decades of the century. Yale was perceived as the institutional nucleus of intellectualism in the state, a place from which Zephaniah benefitted directly and from which the daughters benefitted vicariously. In entries dated August 26, 1813 and September 1, 1813, Julia noted that she had heard President Dwight speak and that "I saw Mr. Brainard, one of my instructors. I was delighted to see him." Six years later when Julia was again in New Haven for commencement, she noted in her diary of August 19, 1819 that she met Mr. Royal Robbins, a minister, who had been her schoolmaster for Latin. (Robbins later became known as the author of textbooks.) This was as close as the daughters would get to a college education since no institution in the country would admit women.

Actually, formal classroom teaching was the least important part of their education. The most important part was reading. First and foremost among their reading was the Bible. The following entry in Julia's diary is an example. "October 20, 1811 I read seventy chapters in the Bible from the eighteenth of second Samuel to the seventh chapter of first Chronicles and I read twelve chapters in the New Testament." At this rate she read the entire Bible at least twice a year, and the New Testament alone four to six times a year.

Two more entries help shed light on these early years: "Wed May 20, 1812, Abby commenced studying Erasmus with me," and "June 15, Did nothing except read in Mr. Locke on the Intellect." Julia kept up this type of intense reading throughout her life, frequently borrowing books from private libraries around town and ordering books through the mail.

In January 1823, Laurilla, then 33 years old, received a letter from Emma Willard asking her to come teach French at her recently established boarding school for girls in Troy, New York. The Troy Female Seminary, which had opened just two years before in 1821, had an enrollment of about 100 girls from leading families in New York, Massachusetts, Vermont, Connecticut, and as far away as Ohio, South Carolina and Georgia. How Emma Willard, like Sarah Pierce, one of the most important female educators of the 19th century, came to hear of the Smiths is unknown, but in the following diary entry Julia did not express any surprise at the request that Laurilla was asked to go to Troy to teach:

> Friday. I got up with the sun. It rained in the night. I have finished the drawers. I have been in the sleigh this afternoon with Cyrinthia. We called at Mrs. Holmes, Mr. Ramsey's, Thankfuls and M. Wheeler's. We found at the post office two letters, one for our grandmother and the other for Laurilla from Mrs. Willard of Troy. She wants my sister Laurilla to come to Troy and live with her and teach French in her school. She wants her to come in six or seven weeks. My sister wants to go.

Laurilla accepted, a decision about which Julia wrote

"I would like it better for her to stay at home with the family but she wants to go. Later on, Laurilla prevailed on Julia to join her there:

> June 26, 1823   Phoeba Ann came home from school and said that there was a letter for me at the post office and I went after it. It was from Laurilla. She wants me to go and live with her. I don't want to but I suppose I will go because my mothers and sisters desire it.

She packed her bags reluctantly, then traveled by stagecoach to Troy where the only bright spot for her seemed to be the presence of her sister Laurilla. She was homesick from the moment she left Glastonbury to the moment she returned for good ten months later. While there, Julia taught French, Latin, and arithmetic, and studied Euclidean geometry, a subject she despised at the beginning. "Friday, July 11, 1823, This evening I went to Mrs. Willard's room to recite Euclid. I did it perfectly. I thoroughly hate it. Saturday July 12, 1823 Arose at five. Studied Euclid and I hate it more and more." But within a few months Julia was teaching Euclid herself. "Tuesday 30 [September 1823] After French class had recited Miss R. Eden came to my chamber to study arithmetic. She spent an hour with me. Miss Cass came here - new scholar. She came last evening. I heard Miss Riker recite Euclid. Spent the afternoon teaching French, Latin and arithmetic."

Emma Willard endeavored to add courses such as geometry and astronomy to her curriculum at Troy but finding qualified teachers was a perpetual, sometimes insurmountable, problem. When she could find no one, she often studied the subject herself, reciting in the evenings to Amos Eaton, a professor of Natural Sciences at Rensselaer

Institute. She then taught the subject to her teachers who would in turn teach the students. This was the pattern that she followed with Julia and Euclidean geometry. But with Julia, Mrs. Willard's work would not yield much fruit in terms of further teaching. Julia was overwhelmingly homesick which led to her being physically ill. Often she complained of headaches and sore throats, for which she frequently took laudanum to relieve the pain. By winter, Julia was most anxious to leave. A brief visit home at Christmas did nothing to quench her desire to quit Troy for good. Even though Emma Willard pleaded with her to stay, offering her $200 per year to teach, she only wanted to return to Glastonbury. Apparently her family was equally happy at the prospect of her return for Hannah wrote her the following light-hearted poem (of which only a portion is printed here), written in Scottish dialect in a style similar to that used by Robert Burns, about all the things that had gone awry in the garden, barnyard, town, and even world because of Julia's absence. Julia received it at Troy on April 16, 1824 according to her diary:

And are ye sure, as weel ye ought
    To be, of coming home
I'm downright dizzy with the thought
    That I shall ye come
I canna read, I canna sing
    I canna write at a'
There is nae luck in ilka thing
    When ye are gone awa'.

The smallpox gaed, around about,
    An our ane doctor blam'd.
Justices met to quell the rout
    And Fansher got defam'd
There is nae luck in our town

Tho' we are bold and braw
There is nae luck upstreet nor down
When ye are gone awa.'

Finally in May, 1824, Julia left Troy, never to return to full-time teaching though Emma Willard tried to coax her to come back the following year. Upon her arrival in Glastonbury, she exclaimed in her diary "Oh, how beautiful it is here. The gardens, the yard, the trees, etc. I will not return to Troy for a long time, if ever." Not long after her return, however, she was once again teaching French to individual students. She also kept up her study of Euclid, even corresponding with a student at Yale who sent her problems to solve.

Laurilla had left Emma Willard's school the previous fall in 1823. She moved to Hartford where she taught French and painted pictures, a hobby she practiced on a semi-professional basis. While there she boarded with a family named Olcott and associated with some of the local literati. In a sketchbook kept by Laurilla in the 1820s, into which friends copied poems and in which she made small pencil and watercolor drawings of Glastonbury houses and landscapes, is a sentimental elegy penned by Harriet Elizabeth Beecher, then only 15 years old, who would become Harriet Beecher Stowe. It is possible that Harriet was a student of Laurilla's since Laurilla was 34 years old at the time. Years later after Laurilla had returned to live in Glastonbury, she built herself a log cabin where she could paint in peace. It was called Uncle Tom's Cabin after the title of Harriet Beecher Stowe's book which was published in 1852.

In her book *The Bonds of Womanhood: "Woman's Sphere" in New England, 1780-1835*, Nancy F. Cott commented on the importance of the female academies and the friendships they helped create:

The philosophy of female education that triumphed by 1820 in New England inclined women to see their destiny as a shared one and to look to one another for similar sensibilities and moral support. By providing both convenient circumstances and a justifying ideology, academies promoted sisterhood among women. Even though most individuals spent only a few months at an academy at a time (perhaps only a few months altogether) the experience attuned them to female friendship with a force out of proportion to its duration.

Although the Smith sisters had many friends outside the immediate family and corresponded with women they had known while attending and teaching at various schools, it was to each other that they turned for moral support. As has been mentioned, none of the sisters ever married except Julia at age 86 following Abby's death. Although there is a story related by a distant relative after their deaths that the sisters made a pact early in life not to marry, there is no indication of such a pact in Julia's diary. Yet although she wrote of enjoying dances and male visitors, the diary is strangely devoid of any romantic interest. Her entries tended to be very quotidian. She commented on the work she had done, what she had read, and who had come to visit, but she rarely commented on political events or local town news even when it directly affected her family. Nor did she express her feelings much, except to say she was happy to see someone or "vexed" at a problem. But it would be an error to assume that such a flat recording of daily activities indicates that Julia had no political, social, or romantic ideas.

Only conjecture is possible as to why the sisters did

not marry. First, they came of age during the first two decades of the nineteenth century when a great exodus to the western part of New York State and Ohio took place from Connecticut, leaving an imbalance in the ratio of males to females. Second, the sisters were better educated than most of the males in Glastonbury, or for that matter, in the entire state of Connecticut, an aspect that would not have been looked on favorably by potential suitors. In short, the Smiths may have educated themselves right out of the marriage market.

Another possibility is raised in an interview with Julia and Abby by Dr. C.C. Dills, dated January 21, 1874. He asked them why they had not married. At first "echo but answered this question," then they apparently explained "that the father had imbibed a prejudice against marriage laws, and a distrust of man's chivalry, while discharging his duties as a lawyer! ...Though the father only exhibited his convictions in a mild and general way by withholding special opportunities for company, and always speaking as if the daughters would remain together, yet it must have had its effect, as no other special cause operated."

Although the fact that the sisters never married is an enigma, the results of that decision are clear and important. In a culture where couples formed the dominant societal structure, and daughters were expected to grow up to become wives and mothers, the sisters' spinsterhood immediately set them apart. Their adult lives settled into a quiet domestic routine. They divided up the housework, with two sisters taking a turn each week. Julia frequently noted that it was her turn to cook in the kitchen, or her turn to clean the chambers, etc.. According to the memoirs of Lillian Prudden, they all wore white dresses which were expected to stay clean for four days with reasonable care, regardless of what chores were assigned:

Each sister had a specialty. The oldest was
musical and for her a piano was imported
about 1820. She was also considered
handsome. On my first visit there in 1870
she played and sang to me with very simple
grace and dignity. She was over 80 then, but
there was a charm in her enjoyment of the
old ballads she had sung in her youth, and
the admiration of her two sisters for the
performance was so genuine that I doubt if
they thought her voice lacked anything.
Cyrinthia Sacretia was a skilled
needlewoman, and the wrought chair back
and screens and ottomans were exhibited
with pride, but "My sister Laurilla's"
portraits of the family and other paintings
were shown with still greater pride in the
artist. Abby said she had no talent, she was
just domestic and she kept house for the
others, but I remember hers as the sweetest
face of all and she was the one who found
out the ambition of the neighbor's child for
education and helped her to get it and to
whom the poor and the unfortunate came for
sympathy. Julia was from the first the
student.

Throughout their lives, they continued to add interest
to interest, always with zealousness. Advancing years did
not diminish their enthusiasms. When the piano arrived
from Meriden, Connecticut, Julia spent hours a day
practicing. In fact, so anxious were the sisters to begin
learning that before it arrived, they marked off keys on a
board and practiced on that. Cyrinthia was a
horticulturalist, as was Abby, keeping notes on what she

planted and reading a publication called *The Cultivator* for advice on how to maximize crops. She also knew the medicinal uses of both wild and cultivated plants, and in one extant note she copied information about the use of iodine to treat goiter. Abby, like her mother, wrote poetry occasionally for her own enjoyment. But next to Julia, the most talented sister was Laurilla. Katherine Hunt, a friend and distant relative, described one of Laurilla's art projects:

> My father presented her with a hatchet which he manufactured and she cut a hickory tree with it and carved from it a miniature Indian group, squaw and pappose, dressed them in Indian costume, blankets, moccasins and so forth, loaded them with baskets and brooms and wrote the poetic appeal they carried in front of them. All from the same creative hand they were perfect masterpieces, much admired, were sold for the benefit of the Abolition cause. If I remember rightly, a Mr. Norton of Farmington paid $150 for them and sent them as a present to Queen Victoria. She, Laurilla, possessed great powers of imitation and a wonderful memory which enabled her to repeat lecture or address verbatim and in every way imitate the speaker so exactly that unless you saw the speaker you might easily be deceived.

There is no doubt that to the more intellectually staid citizens of Glastonbury, the Smith women were considered slightly eccentric at the beginning of the century and very eccentric by the middle. They became a closed society, supportive of each other, sharing chores in the house and farm and encouraging each other in intellectual and social justice pursuits. Had there been only two or three sisters, they might have felt more acutely the cultural pressure to conform to the female "Cult of Domesticity" and chosen passivity on social justice issues. But with six, they gained from each other the strength to withstand the criticism which came their way as a result of their outspoken stands on abolition and suffrage.

In his *Autobiography and Reminiscences*, Henry Titus Welles, who grew up near the Smiths and who was tutored by Julia in French when he was a boy, said that the family:

> did not seem to have a love of the marvelous, nor a desire to be eccentric. But they did have a pride of independence, and arrogated to themselves superior judgment, and were inordinately tenacious of their own opinions. They were self-sufficient. But nevertheless their lives were fragrant with good deeds. They were ever at the bedside of the sick, and were ministering angels to the poor. They were Christians withal, and their record is written in letters of gold in the Lamb's Book of Life, forever and ever.

In 1832, Erastus Salisbury Field, an itinerant portrait painter, came to Glastonbury and painted pictures of the Smiths. All have been lost except that of Zephaniah. Dressed in a black jacket with a prominent collar, a white shirt and cravat, he stares directly out from the canvas, his left hand resting on a law book which is slightly open, as if he had just paused for a moment in the midst of arguing a case. As to the paintings of the sisters, a reporter for the *Nantucket Inquirer and Mirror*, who was a guest of the Smiths in 1874 at the time of the taxation battle, described the impression the portraits had on him:

> In my sleeping apartment I had not
> observed, by the feeble light of the candle,
> that anything but a comfortable bed awaited
> me, till I opened my eyes and the bright
> sunshine fell upon the walls of the room and
> I started up and looked about me; for there
> suspended on every side were the life-size
> portraits of the five sisters gazing at me! all
> in the mutton-leg sleeves, the high-back
> combs, the puffs and ruffs of the olden time:
> -- coming upon me so unexpectedly, and so
> very true to life-size, that whichever way I
> turned their eyes were bent upon me, I was
> fain to beat a hasty retreat, when Miss Abby
> opportunely came to my relief, and in the
> order of their ages, introduced me to the
> sisters..."

Apparently after Julia married and the contents of the house were auctioned off, the portraits made their way into the hands of the Mitchel family in Southbury. After the death of David Hickok, Abigail Hickok married Eleazer Mitchel and there had always been a friendly relationship between the two families. Following Julia's death, a reporter visited the Mitchel household and viewed the portraits which had been hung in the center hall. Hannah, who would have been 65 years old, was painted wearing a stiff frilled cap. Cyrinthia Lucretia was "black-haired and slender-fingered as are all the sisters," who he thought beautiful.

The sense of domestic serenity and stability which had always surrounded the daughters was shattered the day after Christmas in 1835. Late on the evening of December

26, Zephaniah slipped on the ice between the house and barn and broke his thigh. The doctor was summoned immediately but the break was so bad that he could not set it until the next day. Although the family tended him zealously and the doctor came daily, Zephaniah never recovered and died five weeks later at the age of 77 apparently of a head injury received in the same fall. On February 1, 1836, Julia entered in her diary:

> As I write our father is no more. He died at nine o'clock this morning. Can we bear it. But he went without a murmur. God was very merciful to my father for he did not suffer in his last moments. Mrs. Hollister and Deacon Hale were with us in that sad hour. Our other friends have been here. Jean Moseley, Thomas Watrous, Deacon Hale and Mr. Riddel have performed the last offices. Priscilla Lockwood has spent the day with us. We no longer have our father. We have been with him so long it is almost unbearable to think of it.

Without any close male relative, the Smith women would come to feel Zephaniah's loss keenly as the years passed. Besides the fact that they loved him very much and mourned his death, his passing also meant that they had no one to vote in their stead or speak for them in front of legislative bodies. In a secure position financially, they were in a tenuous position culturally, as were all widows and single women during this era. "O this is a family without a husband, without a father, without a brother, without an uncle, without a man who has the care of us" lamented Julia a few days after his death. As a male legislator, lawyer and town leader, Zephaniah had been the one family member out in the world, so to speak, a man whose professional friendships included leaders in the state, and whose career took him on frequent trips around the Hartford area. Glastonbury may have been rural but the Smiths were cosmopolitan largely because of Zephaniah's career. Unlike the ministry, law was a congenial profession for him, one in which his agile mind could question and probe without fear of committing religious heresy; yet it was his brief spell as a minister which left the deepest impression on his daughters.

"For Jehovah shall know
the way of the just."
Psalm 1: 6

5

RELIGION:
THE WAY OF THE JUST

One aspect of culture that never ceased to amaze Alexis de Tocqueville, the peripatetic and prescient French commentator on American life during the early 1830s, was the enormous part religion played in all parts of society. In *Democracy in America*, he wrote:

> Religion in America takes no direct part in the government of society, but nevertheless it must be regarded as the foremost of the political institutions of that country; for if it does not impart a taste for freedom, it facilitates the use of free institutions. Indeed, it is in this same point of view that

the inhabitants of the United States themselves look upon religious belief. I do not know whether all the Americans have a sincere faith in their religion, for who can search the human heart? But I am certain that they hold it to be indispensable to the maintenance of republican institutions. This opinion is not peculiar to a class of citizen or to a party, but it belongs to the whole nation, and to every rank of society.

To understand the Smiths, it must be realized that although their form of belief in God took a peculiar turn, the fact that they let belief shape their entire lives was common. As de Tocqueville observed, the importance of religion was "not peculiar to a class of citizen or to a party, but it belongs to the whole nation, and to every rank of society." There was not a major social issue which was not analyzed ad nauseam theologically. Temperance, the role of women, even the emigration westward and Manifest Destiny were as much religious subjects as they were social and cultural. But it was slavery which received the most extensive religious scrutiny. Proof-texting slavery, both pro and con, was carried on all across the nation and not only by ministers. Politicians of all persuasions continually inserted religious language into their speeches. Henry Clay could with deep sincerity say in a speech before Congress in December 1838 that:

It has been [God's] divine pleasure to make the black man black and the white man white, and to distinguish them by other repulsive constitutional differences. It is not necessary for me to maintain, nor shall I endeavor to prove, that it was any part of

His divine intention that the one race should
be held in perpetual bandage [sic] by the
other; but this I say, that those whom he has
created different, and has declared, by their
physical stature and color, ought to be kept
asunder, should not be brought together by
any process whatever of unnatural
amalgamation.

This was not mere rhetoric on Clay's part. It was a
profoundly held belief that he shared with thousands upon
thousands of others. It is small wonder that the Civil War
was so virulent, for its soldiers were driven not only by
different secular conceptions of how society should be
structured but by different theological visions.

The major social causes of the antebellum era,
including temperance and moral reform were all fueled by
similar sentiments. As will be discussed, the Second Great
Awakening, which swept the country during the first part
of the nineteenth century, would lead to disagreements as
to how religion should be expressed, but not about the fact
that the Republic was under God. That was assumed by the
nation -- and by the Smiths.

Although Zephaniah had left the ministry, he did not
break entirely with the Congregational Church, nor did he
and his family break from the thinking of Robert
Sandeman. Throughout the first two decades of the
nineteenth century, the family attended the First Society in
Glastonbury located not far from their home on Main
Street. Hannah even helped search for a new minister in
March 1804 after the Reverend William Lockwood had to
resign because of ill health. They also occasionally attended
the Episcopal Church in town and followed closely what
was happening on the religious front in the other
denominations. On May 23, 1810, Julia wrote to her

grandmother Abigail Mitchel:

> You desire to know if the awakening
> continues in Glastenbury [sic] there are a
> number of people who have joined the
> church from the upper and lower parts of
> the town but none that I am particularly
> acquainted with. Mr. Hawes has conference
> twice a week which are generally full. We
> have all sorts of people here, and a number
> of Universalists. They had a meeting last
> sabbath. Mr. Eben Strong was in town and
> attended. The Methodists have meetings on
> the green very often and attract a great deal
> of attention and there is scarce a family but
> goes to hear them.

In her diary, Julia exhibited an interest in other forms
of faith as well. On May 17, 1817, Julia and Zephina
visited New York City, having come by boat down the
Hudson River. The next day Julia wrote "Sunday 18, It
rained a little in the morning. I went to the brick
Presbyterian church with Mr. Isham and Eliza. Zephina
stayed aboard the vessel. In the afternoon Zephina went
with us to the Roman Catholic Church -- it was a great
curiosity for us."

Of greater significance is that during the second decade
Julia began to read the works of John Glas and Robert
Sandeman. By 1823 when Julia was teaching at Emma
Willard's school in Troy, New York, she no longer
attended church. Entries similar to the following continue
for several years. "Sunday 21 [July 1822] Read the Bible
and Mr. Glas almost all day. Finished the Old and New
Testament once more. Hot." On October 6, 1822, Julia
even attended a Sandemanian meeting in Newtown at the

house of Dr. Shepherd, a man with whom she had corresponded several times. She remarked "They read the sacred scriptures, and prayed and talked, etc., and we were very content with it."

While at Emma Willard's school, Julia was invited to visit with some cousins who lived in the nearby community of Greenville, New York. Greenville, as was Troy, was located in an area which would eventually be called the "Burned Over District" due to the number of revivals and the heat of the religious ferment that occurred there during the Second Great Awakening. Although Julia had looked forward to the visit, she soon found her religious views under attack:

> Sunday 10 [August 1823] Got up before six. It is a strange thing to the family that I do not attend church. They do not like it, but I cannot go. They went to what they call a Revival. I read the Bible. It rained some this afternoon.

One week later the cousins were apparently pressuring her to attend:

> Sunday 17 [August 1823] Arose around six. David Hickok, one of my cousins, came over to see me in the morning. The whole family went to church except the little colored one and myself. I read the Bible. Emelisse Hall came over from church to spend the night. David Hickok spent the evening here. The others went to church except Merilla. My cousin talked about religion with me until eleven o'clock. He wanted to persuade me to go to church.

The next week she left her cousins' home on Saturday, perhaps to avoid another confrontation on Sunday about church attendance. For all her loneliness at Emma Willard's seminary in Troy, she was happy to return. As for the beliefs of the rest of the family, Zephaniah's funeral in 1836 was conducted by Deacon Hale and Reverend Samuel Riddel, the minister of First Congregational Church, indicating at least a tenuous connection to the institutional church, but by the 1840's a major schism did indeed occur. In 1842 at least Julia and Abby became involved with Millerism. A Vermont farmer, William Miller claimed that in 1843 Jesus Christ would appear in the clouds. He would raise up the righteous dead and, together with the righteous living, they would be caught up to meet Him in the air. After the earth was purified by fire and the souls of the damned were sent to hell, the saints would return to earth to reign with Jesus for one thousand years. Studying the Biblical prophecy in the Book of Daniel, "Unto two thousand and three hundred days; then shall the sanctuary be cleansed," Miller calculated that the Second Coming would occur in 1843, later recalculated to 1844. Thousands of people across New England and New York waited for that day in great agitation stirred up in part by Miller's numerous sermons (he preached over 300 times in one six-month period) and those of the approximately 200 ministers and 500 public lecturers who were converted by Miller's vision of the Second Coming:

> I am satisfied that the end of the world is at hand. The evidence flows in from every quarter...soon, very soon, God will arise in his anger and the vine of the earth will be reaped. See! See! -- the angel with his sharp sickle is about to take the field! See yonder trembling victims fall before his pestilential

breath! High and low, rich and poor,
trembling and falling before the appalling
grave, the dreadful cholera...Behold, the
heavens grow black with clouds; the sun has
veiled himself; the moon, pale and forsaken,
hangs in middle air; the hail descends; the
seven thunders utter loud their voices; the
lightnings send their vivid gleams and
sulphurous flames abroad; the great city of
the nations falls to rise no more forever and
forever! At this dread moment, look! The
clouds have burst asunder; the heavens
appear; the great white throne is in sight!
Amazement fills the Universe with awe! He
comes! -- He comes! -- Behold the Savior
comes! -- Lift up your hands, ye saints --
He comes! He comes! He comes!

Apart from those who openly declared themselves to
be Millerites, there were many people who followed the
happenings associated with William Miller closely. For
each person who dismissed Miller as a charlatan gathering
a band of half-crazed followers, there was someone else
who was quietly curious and a little concerned about the
state of his or her own soul if the end of the world were
imminent. In his article entitled "Millerites," David Rowe,
a noted scholar of the movement, points out that:

many orthodox Christians accepted Miller's
tenets and used millenarian-like rhetoric
without ever joining the Adventist
movement. Millerism's conscious pietism
and evangelicalism and its profitable
recourse to the popular revivalism of the day
as its principal vehicle of propagation not

> only encouraged commitment to Adventism;
> it also 'interested' many professing
> Christians who found the Millerites' beliefs
> and rhetoric familiar and comfortable but
> who would have been shocked had anyone
> called them "Millerites."

Joseph Wright, who lived approximately a mile north of the Smiths on Main Street, recorded in his diary at the end of December that 1842 had been the worst year for farming in his entire life with both yield and prices much reduced. A hard-working, successful farmer as well as a respected church leader at First Church, his dismay at the state of the economy and the political malaise of the entire country is indicative of what other Glastonbury farm families, including the Smiths, must have been thinking and feeling:

> The embarrassment of the country in its
> finances and business have been
> unprecedented. The currency is deranged
> and confidence in men is exceedingly
> impaired. Banks have failed in many
> instances and instead of an expanded
> currency, it is now greatly contracted....I
> never found myself in such embarrassed and
> discouraging circumstances in my life, and
> it seems if the country does not improve in
> business and general prosperity, we shall
> many of us have to make terrible sacrifices.

It is exactly in such unstable times that interest in the apocalyptic increases. If Joseph Wright, a most pragmatic Yankee, could speak of the possible need for "terrible sacrifices," it is not hard to assume that others in town had begun to watch the heavens for signs and search their souls for blemish. To heighten the sense of ominous expectation, a brilliant comet blazed across the sky in 1842, a sure precursor according to the believers.

As a Sandemanian, Julia's religious beliefs were anti-clerical and centered on Christ, specifically that it was his sacrifice on the cross alone which bought salvation for believers, not personal belief or good works. She also believed in the "bare" power of the Bible which each person on his or her own could accept or reject. Miller also encouraged people to study the Bible and draw their own conclusions. There was a strong individualistic, egalitarian streak in both Sandemanianism and Millerism which may have predisposed Julia to accept Miller's predictions as true. After all, Zephaniah himself had spoken with passion in one of his sermons of Christ being "revealed from heaven with his holy angels in flaming fire." At the end of 1842, Julia's diary is filled with references to Miller and his writings which she and Abby had been studying daily. The last entry of that year reads:

> Monday 31 [December 1842] I have stayed in the house all the day except I have been walking in the afternoon in order to see Henry Welles. I read the Bible almost all day. I've eaten nothing since yesterday noon. It is the last day of the year, perhaps all of us should be prepared to enter the new year 1843 which according to Mr. Miller could be the last year of this world. That the Great Lord might give us faith to be always ready for the Second Coming.

Paradoxically, that is the last entry in her entire diary. After keeping it for 32 years in French, from this point on she entered only meteorological data in English with an entry about the death of Laurilla on March 19, 1857. Since Christ was to appear in the clouds, heralded by strange phenomena in nature, such as the spectacular comet which appeared in 1842, a meteorological journal was a very apt thing for a believer to keep. Julia herself never admitted in later life that she and her sisters became followers of Miller. There were believers in Glastonbury and, in fact, a Seventh Day Adventist Church was formed a few years after what would be called the "Great Disappointment," but facts are scarce in part because some believers were ashamed to acknowledge their involvement in what amounted to a religious debacle. There are two second-hand accounts of the Smiths' involvement in Millerism. The first was written by Henry Titus Welles in his *Autobiography and Reminiscences*. Welles had grown up less than a quarter mile from the Smiths and had walked over there frequently when in his teens to study French under Julia and had stayed in touch with her until the end of her life. Given his knowledge, fondness and respect for the Smiths, his description can be relied upon. Welles said that after they espoused the doctrines of Miller, they "renounced all human authority in religious doctrine, insisted on a hidden sense in the Bible which they could see but which they could not communicate, gave up everything that suggested a love of the world, turning the pictures to the wall, covering the piano with a pall, and putting the plants in the cellar." Another memoir written by Mary T. Hale also states that the sisters let their plants die and turned their pictures to the wall, and adds that they had ascension robes laid out in readiness for the second coming of Christ. However, both of these memoirs were written long after the Smiths had died. Therefore, the only thing which is known with certainty about the Smiths' involvement with Millerism is that following the failure of

Miller's predictions, Julia and Abby turned to the Bible to
determine the scriptural validity of those predictions.
Because of Julia's knowledge of Greek and Latin, they
could read several versions of the New Testament, but they
felt stymied in reading the Old Testament because all they
had available to them was the King James Version. Miller
had also relied upon the King James Version in working
out his chronology which culminated in 1843 or 1844.
Since the world had not ended, but Miller's math seemed
to be correct, then perhaps the error was in the translation.
Could it be that the true meaning of God's word had been
occluded by well-meaning but inept translators and
interpreters? Miller himself felt that the interpreters were
to blame. Discouraged after the Great Disappointment, he
concluded "I was misled in my calculations; not by the
words of God, nor by the established principles of
interpretation I adopted, but by the authorities which I
followed in history and chronology." Without knowing
Greek and Latin as did Julia Smith, he did not perceive that
the translation itself might be at fault. As Julia stated in the
preface to her translation, she and her sisters:

> saw by the margin that the text had not been
> given literally, and it was the literal meaning
> we were seeking. I had studied Latin and
> Greek at school, and began by translating
> the Greek New Testament, and then the
> Septuagint, from which our Savior quoted
> one or two texts which are not in the
> Hebrew Bible, and there is now said to be
> no Hebrew Bible extant so old as the
> Septuagint. We all had a strong desire to
> learn the significance of the proper names,
> and I wrote to a learned friend about it, and
> he advised me to study Hebrew saying "it

was a simple language and easily learned,
there being but one book in the world of
pure Hebrew, which was the Bible."

The learned friend to whom Julia referred was Samuel
Jarvis, an Episcopal minister in Middletown, Connecticut,
from whom she had occasionally borrowed books to
translate. Jarvis had one of the best libraries in the state,
indeed one of the best in the country. Prior to assuming the
pulpit in Middletown, he had been a professor at Trinity
College in Hartford (then known as Washington College),
and prior to that he and his family had lived for several
years in Europe, where he had indulged his passion for
acquiring choice books. So renowned was his collection,
numbering between 8,000 and 10,000 volumes, that when
it was auctioned off after his death, institutions in Europe
as well as in the United States submitted bids. Among the
Bibles he possessed were the Complutensian Antwerp,
London and Paris Polyglot, Cranmer's and the Bishops'
Bibles, Tyndale's Pentateuch, a fragment of Erasmus'
paraphrase of the New Testament (1548), a late Breeches
or Geneva version (London 1606), and the first volume of
the Douay (1601). Whether Jarvis loaned Julia any of his
valuable manuscripts is not known, but what is clear is that
she set about the task of learning Hebrew with the same
singlemindedness she had earlier applied to Greek and
Latin. According to one account, she would become so
immersed in the process of translation that she often did
not hear the dinner bell and had to be reminded by her
sisters to eat.

Then began eight years of concentrated effort (from
1847 to 1855). During this prolonged period, Julia met
weekly with her sisters and a close friend named Emily
Moseley to study what her work had so far revealed. She
read from small, hand-bound folios, which would

eventually contain over 10,000 neatly written pages. The influence of her sister Abby was probably the greatest at these meetings. In fact, Abby often referred to the project as "our" Bible. By 1855, Julia had translated the Bible not once but five times in its entirety, each time striving to come nearer the original meaning. In her words:

> [I] wrote it out word for word, giving no ideas of my own, but endeavoring to put the same English word for the same Hebrew or Greek word, everywhere, while King James translators have wholly differed from this rule; but it appeared to us to give a much clearer understanding of the text...It may be thought by the public in general, that I have great confidence in myself, in not conferring with the learned in so great a work, but as there is but one book in the Hebrew tongue, and I have defined it word for word, I do not see how anybody can know more about it than I do. It being a dead language no improvements can be made upon it.

Although the Smith sisters had already sundered their ties to First Church, Emily Moseley, their close friend and fellow Bible student had not. But so convinced did Emily Moseley become of the correctness of the Smith's theology that she herself was excommunicated from First Church in 1844. Although excommunication from Congregational churches was not an uncommon occurrence during this era, being meted out for drunkenness, lack of attendance, and various other infractions, Emily's excommunication shook the members of First Church because in no uncertain terms she ripped their theology to shreds. Joseph Wright gave a fascinating account of that occurrence in his diary:

> 1844 Sept. 1 Communion. Emily Moseley
> was excommunicated from the church for
> abstaining from the communion and publick
> worship and for holding such errors as
> these, viz, that the church is antichrist and
> no better than popery mohametanism or
> paganism, that the christian ministry is an
> usurpation, the sabbath no better than any
> other day, there is no obligation on
> christians to send missionaries abroad or to
> labor for the conversion of sinners, the bible
> is all that is needed to guide us to heaven
> etc. We were all shocked to see to what
> lengths she had gone in her delusions.

There are the marks of Sandemanian theology throughout Wright's listing: that ministers, missionaries and other church workers were unnecessary, that the Bible was all that was needed, and that the church itself had drifted so far from correct theology that it was no better than paganism. Sandemanianism as an organized sect may have died out, but in 1844 it could claim at least one new convert.

Julia had not set about preparing her translation with any intention of having it published. Like so many other projects that the Smiths undertook, it was for her own personal edification. It was not until her tax battle with the Town of Glastonbury in the 1870s that she decided to have it published at her own expense in order to prove the intellectual superiority of women, at which point it would come to the attention of Elizabeth Cady Stanton and other suffragists. But at the time she was translating, Julia's only goal was to reach the true meaning of the words, unsullied by the innate prejudices and acquired beliefs of the translator.

Julia's most radical departure from tradition was to use the future rather than the past tense in the Old Testament historical narratives. Certain passages thus achieve a startling presentness, as if the events are ongoing or about to take place. Disconcertingly, she also changed tenses, from future to past to future as is apparent in her translation of Genesis 1: 3-5:

> And God will say there shall be light, and there shall be light. And God will see the light that it is good, and God will separate between the light and between the darkness. And God will call to the light day, and to the darkness he called night: and the evening shall be, and the morning shall be one day.

In the preface to her translation, Julia explained her rationale for the frequent shift in tenses, linking it to the 2 Corinthians scripture which was of overriding importance to her:

> It is very possible that the readers of this book may think it strange that I have made such use of the tenses, going according to the Hebrew grammar. It seems that the original Hebrew had no regard to time, and that the Bible speaks for all ages. If I did not follow the tenses as they are, I myself should be the judge, and man must not be trusted with regard to the Word of God. I think the promiscuous use of the tense shows that there must be something hidden, that we must search out, and not hold to the outward for the "letter kills, but the Spirit gives life."

Julia made other changes in an effort to return to what she considered to be the original, pure text. She preferred the name "Jehovah" to "Lord" and "God." She translated the name Eve as "life." She also substituted the word "love" for the word "charity" in 1 Corinthians 13. So also, she used the word "immerse" instead of "baptize," i.e. "John the Immerser." Here at least she may have let her own Sandemanian bent decide her word choice, whether consciously or unconsciously, for Sandeman advocated immersion. A good example of Julia's tenacious dedication to the original language is her disjointed translation of Psalm 77, a psalm that has always presented great difficulties for translators because of its archaic language.

> Will Jehovah reject forever? and will he no more add to be satisfied? Did his mercy fail forever? his word come to an end to generation and generation? Did God forget to compassionate? or in anger did he gather his compassions? Silence. And saying, This has made me sick: the years of the right hand of the Most High. I will remember the works of Jah: for I will remember the ancient time of thy wonder. And I meditated in all thy work, and I will think upon all thy doings. O God, thy way is in the holy place: what God great as God? Thou the God doing wonder: thou didst make known thy strength among the peoples. Thou didst redeem with thy arm thy people the sons of Jacob and Joseph. Silence.

Although recent philological studies, including insights gained from Ugaritic, have helped somewhat to clarify the meaning of the words in this complex psalm, Julia herself did not see any problems with linguistic obscurities because she felt that meaning came as much through divine revelation as through intellectual understanding. She stated in the preface to the Bible that "The whole construction is so complete, that it does seem to be the work of inspiration, and the only communication from God to man, for all time. The work is given in types, in figures, in parables, and in dark sayings, a knowledge of which is gained, as all other knowledge is gained, by the desire of the heart to learn it." The Bible was, in short, not like other books. It was not only divinely inspired, it was divinely charged. The words were not an endpoint in themselves; they did not hold the ultimate meaning. The words were instead a conduit by which God could speak to believers in a way which surpassed language. This being the case, Julia considered that it was pure hubris for a translator to smooth out the sentences; to do so was to take on the trappings of a god; to do so was sin.

However, not all of Julia's translation was syntactically fractured. Generally her New Testament reveals that she had a firmer command of Greek and Latin than of Hebrew, and thus is more fluid, exemplified by her wording of the Lord's Prayer:

> Therefore, so do ye pray: Our Father which in the heavens, Let thy name be declared holy. Let thy kingdom come. Let thy will be as in heaven also upon the earth. Give us this day our bread sufficient for sustenance and let go to us our debts, as we let go to our debtors. And thou shouldst not lead us into temptation, but deliver thou us from evil. For thine is the kingdom, and the power, and the glory, forever. Amen.

Many passages, however, remain difficult to read due to a halting awkwardness -- an awkwardness which was derived not from ineptitude but faith. Julia knew that two languages never correspond exactly, that idioms tied to one culture lose meaning, or even worse, convey the wrong meaning when translated word for word, but she believed that these principles did not apply to Bible translation. Julia was not alone in holding this belief; in fact, it was the rule rather than the exception during the Victorian era. In his book *Translating the Bible*, Frederick C. Grant discusses why the Anglican Church in England felt compelled to appoint a committee in 1870 to undertake the first official revision of the Bible. The King James Version:

> irked the Victorian scholars whose minds had been trained in a "literal" rendering of the classics and were now being subjected to the increasing pressure of "scientific" conceptions of learning, with measurable exactitude set up as a standard and norm for all writing and translation. There were also theological conceptions at work in men's minds. There *must* be standard text of the New Testament; an inspired book *must* have a "neutral" text, to be found in certain manuscripts, uninfluenced by the host of variations in others. There *must* be a precise theological significance attaching to each theological term used, and every author *must* be self-consistent...Otherwise, divine revelation, and the inspiration of Holy Scripture, would not be fully assured.

It is interesting to note that the Authorized Revised Version printed in 1885 also failed to win the favor of readers for exactly the same reasons as Julia's translation failed. For all its supposed exactitude, it lacked grace of the human kind, and without it, it lacked the ability to inspire. Not until 1953 and the release of the Revised Standard Version would the dominance of the King James Version be threatened.

There was only one postscript of note to Julia's translation. Elizabeth Cady Stanton, like many other suffragettes, was deeply disturbed by what she perceived to be the anti-female bias in the Bible. Spurred on in part by Julia's translation, she formed a committee, including Lucy Stone, Frances Ellen Burr, and Matilda Joslyn Gage, to name a few, that published a commentary called *The Woman's Bible*. The Revising Committee used Julia's Bible as their ultimate scriptural authority. In acknowledging that debt, Frances Ellen Burr wrote in the appendix:

> Julia Smith's translation of the Bible stands out unique among all translations. It is the only one ever made by a woman, and the only one, it appears, ever made by man or woman without help. Wycliff, "the morning star of the Reformation," made a translation from the Vulgate, assisted by Nicholas of Hereford. He was not sufficiently familiar with Hebrew and Greek to translate from those tongues. Coverdale's translation was not done alone. In his dedication to the king he says he has humbly followed his interpreters and that under correction. Tyndale, in his translation, had the assistance of Frye, of William Roye, and also of Miles Coverdale. Julia Smith translated the whole Bible absolutely alone.

Even though Julia's translation is considered the first suffragist Bible, it cannot be used as a template by present-day biblical scholars endeavoring to substitute non-sexist language. In translating the Divine Word, her interest was in the "divine," not in the "word." Had she lived, Julia would probably have been pleased by Elizabeth Cady Stanton's use of her Bible, but she would have felt commentary was unnecessary since meaning did not reside in the language itself.

An article by Carroll Smith-Rosenberg called "The Cross and the Pedestal: Women, Anti-Ritualism and the Emergence of the American Bourgeoisie" helps put the Smiths' religious views into perspective and helps link them to abolitionism. She states that though male clerics and reformers led the Second Great Awakening, which swept in waves across the country during the first half of the nineteenth century, through sheer numbers women dominated the revivals and spiraling church membership:

> Silenced in Christian churches since the days of Paul, women now seized sacred space...Male religious rebels actively encouraged these enthusiastic women. They called on them to organize prayer meetings, to criticize ministers opposed to revivals, to leave their homes and go forth into the byways of the cities to perfect the world...To implement their newfound sacred and social responsibilities more effectively, many respectable women moved beyond individually inspired behavior to form a score of untraditional -- indeed iconoclastic -- organizations...Still others, espousing William Lloyd Garrison's anarchistic message, assumed controversial roles within

the   American   Anti-Slavery   Society.
Temperance and abolitionist women asserted
their right to speak publicly, to hold office
in male organizations, to petition state and
federal legislators, all in the name of a
higher inner light.

Although the Smiths did not participate directly in
activities related to the Second Great Awakening, their
belief in the doctrines of Glas and Sandeman definitely put
them in the same theological arena. The main thrust of the
Second Great Awakening was that salvation depended only
on personal piety and faith. This broke the strangle-hold of
Calvinism with its stern doctrine of predestination. It also
broke the strangle-hold of the institutional church and its
ordained ministers. No longer were sinners quite so
helpless in the hands of an angry God. The theology of the
Second Great Awakening was also perfectionistic. As
espoused by Charles Grandison Finney and other revivalist
ministers, this led to the belief that society could be
reformed. Indeed, if a Christian had faith and worked hard,
heaven could be recreated on Earth. Such an attitude
spawned many social causes. Not surprisingly, most of the
leaders of the American Anti-Slavery Society, including
Theodore Weld and the Tappan brothers, were products of
the Second Great Awakening.

The idea of perfectibility also carried over into
people's personal lives in this period leading to a
heightened interest in hygiene and medicine. Such
movements as Grahamism and hydropathy, also known as
the water cure (in which Cyrinthia participated in a futile
attempt to save her own life) had their roots in the idea of
perfectibility as much as abolition and temperance did. But
perfectibility exacted a high psychological cost. The
popular prophecies of William Miller concerning the years

1843 and 1844 when the earth and its sinful inhabitants were to be destroyed by fire and the righteous believers were to be saved by Christ were but the idea of perfectibility turned inside out.

The perplexing question is why would abolitionists bent on freeing people from slavery in the here and now be attracted to Millerism at all, with its single-minded, single-purpose mission of preparing for the end. Why was Miller himself an abolitionist as was his co-leader Joshua V. Himes. Ronald D. Graybill in his article "The Abolitionist-Millerite Connection" offers some intriguing answers which speak directly to the Smiths' involvement:

> True, abolitionism tended away from the literalism of William Miller's biblical interpretations. Biblical literalism had proven all too useful in the hands of proslavery ministers who defended slavery from the Old and New Testaments. But although Miller's hermeneutic was, on its face, very literalistic and conservative, he carried it so far as to break with conservative prophetic interpretations of his day. Thus he ended up with a psychologically daring and expansive interpretation which appealed to abolitionists like Angelina Grimke Weld, who knew her Bible well but had little respect for orthodox interpretation.

Graybill also maintains that the factional squabbles that ripped apart the American Anti-Slavery Society in the early 1840s led to discouragement among abolitionists that the slaves would ever be freed by organized means. "To reformers, sickened and disappointed by factionalism among abolitionists, the Advent movement offered a thriving, growing, unified alternative. Far from seeming impractical, to many of them it seemed to offer a very tangible and dramatic definition for the word 'immediate' in immediate abolition."

From Graybill's insightful study, it is possible to see that the Smiths' involvement in Millerism was not aberrant; it was not a theological side trip that led nowhere; instead, it was part of a seamless whole. The lives of the Smiths were based on the Bible; when that Bible seemed to fail them, they set out to discover why, and the result was Julia's translations. So also abolition, with which they would be profoundedly involved from the 1830s through the Civil War, was a result of their interpretation of the will of God. For the Smiths, faith always culminated in action, and action culminated in deeper faith.

"Not so the unjust; but as the chaff which the wind shall drive away."
Psalm 1:4

6

THE CULTURAL ROOTS OF THE SMITHS' ABOLITIONISM

Many of the histories of the anti-slavery movement place the reasons for its development on the Christian tradition, the spirit of the Declaration of Independence, the ferment of Jacksonian democracy and the growth of romanticism. David Donald in his essay "Toward a Reconsideration of Abolition" looked at these reasons and asked why the first two at least did not manifest themselves several decades earlier. What was there about the 1830's that compelled anti-slavery to become the cause of choice? In an attempt to find answers, Donald drew a composite picture of Northern abolitionists: they were born between 1790 and 1810 in rural New England of educated, Federalist parents, and most were troubled by spiritual discontent. Donald then concluded that the underlying reason for their impassioned involvement was that their social class was losing primacy to a mercantile bourgeoisie. "Leadership of humanitarian reform may have been influenced by revivalism or by British precedent, but its true origin lay in the drastic dislocation of Northern society."

Donald's description fits the Smiths exactly; it is as if he had taken them as his quintessential example. However, his conclusion is too sweeping, principally because he studied only the leaders of the abolition movement and then made the assumption that his generalizations about the leaders held for the rank-and-file members of the movement as well. Part of the problem is that it is easier to study people who have power because they tend to leave behind diaries, speeches, articles, and books by or about themselves. Mill workers who signed anti-slavery petitions did not leave detailed letters about their rationale for doing so. The black abolitionists who accounted for three-quarters of the 2,300 subscribers to the *Liberator* in April 1834 (just three years after the first issue) generally did not write speeches on the relationship between the state of their souls and the state of the nation. This oversight involves the Smiths because they did not stay neatly within their own social strata when campaigning for abolition and later on for suffrage. They took their anti-slavery petitions and newspapers to the workers who were laboring in the dreary textile mills that lined Roaring Brook in South Glastonbury -- mills which relied for their profitability in part on the low cost of raw cotton raised by slaves. Whereas some white abolitionists eschewed any social contact with blacks, preferring them in the abstract, the Smiths welcomed black abolitionist leaders into their home. The extent of the Smiths' race and class egalitarianism is made manifest by a comment of Julia's during the suffrage battle. It seems that the men in Glastonbury raised the objection that if suffrage were extended to all women it would "let in all the Catholic women and other good for nothing working women." Julia responded "We say, 'do right and let the heavens fall,' leave the consequences with God." She felt that the vote would be of even greater importance to the working woman who had no rights to her own pay, often being forced to sacrifice it to a drunken husband.

Fortunately, some excellent work has been done to correct the misconception that all abolitionists were middle class professionals suffering from religious dyspepsia who eschewed contact with the laboring class. More recent work by Benjamin Quarles (1969), Carroll Smith-Rosenberg (1985), Aileen Kraditor (1967), and David Swift (1989) has helped in this respect. Especially important is the work done by Edward Magdol whose book *The Antislavery Rank and File: A Social Profile of the Abolitionists' Constituency* was published posthumously in 1986. Magdol analyzed some of the abolitionist petitions which were signed by hundreds of thousands of people in the 1830's and 1840's. Specifically, he chose to scrutinize the petitions signed in the following manufacturing cities: Utica, Rome and Schenectady in New York; Fall River, Lynn, Springfield, Worcester and Lowell in Massachusetts. His exhaustive analysis yielded a rich trove of valuable information:

> The people who signed antislavery petitions made up a grand coalition of social groups for reform. The men and women in the antislavery campaign lived in all parts of the cities and in their nearby countryside. They came from all walks of life. Their varied occupations, from "agent" to "wool grader," were listed under at least 120 out of a possible 212 classifications used in this

study. They varied in age from eighteen
years to eighty. Most were born in the states
in which they lived at the time of signing;
some were born in neighboring states. The
large number of petitioners who could not
be found suggests the marked transiency of
the American people. The overwhelming
portion of the petitioners -- from 60 to 70
percent -- owned no real estate. If they did
own property, it tended to be real estate
assessed at between $1,000 and $5,000.
Seventy percent of the petitioners owned no
personal property of assessable value. Those
who did have taxable possessions tended to
fall in the low bracket of $101 to $500.

Magdol's astute conclusion that the educated sons and
daughters of the old mercantile families with deep roots in
their communities joined with the new energetic
manufacturing class in the anti-slavery movement is borne
out by the Smiths. Abolition was not an influential fringe
movement made up of educated malcontents. It crossed
both race and class lines.

There is yet another difficulty with David Donald's
theory on the social class and motivation of abolitionists.
By emphasizing a psychological interpretation of cultural
change, Donald de-emphasized the fact that the institution
of slavery in America itself had undergone an ominous
change since the beginning of the nineteenth century, a
change that troubled New Englanders whether or not they
were abolitionists. At the Constitutional Convention in
1786, the principal goal of the delegates was to create a
union which had a chance of survival. Any proposal on
emancipation would have meant that the southern states
would have abruptly pulled out, dooming the union at its

start. Struggling to find a way to hold the fragile but feisty infant nation together, the delegates came up with the Three-Fifths Compromise which for the purposes of apportionment of representation and taxes stipulated that a Negro was considered to be three-fifths human and two-fifths property, comparable to a beast of burden. At the same time Congress set a twenty-year limit on the importation of slaves. In the minds of many delegates was the hope that over that period slavery would wither away. Unfortunately, by the time the twenty-year limit was up in 1806, no withering had occurred. In fact, even with the ban in international slave trade in place, the "peculiar institution," as Southerners euphemistically labelled slavery, grew stronger. This occurred during the same period that slaves were freed by law in the northern states, slave uprisings in the Caribbean had already led to independent governments, and emancipation movements picked up steam in Great Britain and France. Essentially, the South was moving in a direction diametrically opposite to the rest of the western world. One of the reasons for this paradox, as has been pointed out numerous times by historians of the antebellum era, was the burgeoning northern and European textile industry. Mills needed cotton, which could now be harvested more easily due to Eli Whitney's cotton gin, and cotton -- that labor-intensive monster of a crop -- demanded slaves. Cotton also demanded more and more land because it depleted the soil in which it was grown. In the United States, the stage was set between the North and the South for a massive confrontation over western lands.

In his book *The Peculiar Institution: Slavery in the Ante-bellum South*, Kenneth M. Stampp wrote:

> By the 1830's the fateful decision had been
> made. Slavery, now an integral part of the

southern way of life, was to be preserved,
not as a transitory evil, an unfortunate
legacy of the past, but as a permanent
institution -- a positive good. To think of
abolition was an idle dream. Now even
native Southerners criticized the peculiar
institution at their peril. Finally by the
1830s slavery had assumed the rigidity of an
entrenched institution. It no longer had the
plasticity -- the capacity to modify its shape
-- that it had in the colonial period. Slavery
had crystallized; its form was fixed.

Making the entire picture even more bleak was the fact
that in some areas of the South, though not in all, slavery
had reached a new level of brutality and inhumanity. In the
eighteenth century there had been large gangs of slaves
working in the pestilential lowland rice fields of South
Carolina under undeniably terrible conditions, but generally
the average number of slaves per owner was much smaller
than on the cotton plantations of the nineteenth century.
The very size of these plantations made overseers
necessary. Furthermore, with the constant movement of
white southerners westward in search of new land to
replace exhausted land, slave families were uprooted more
often than had previously been the case. According to
Stampp:

Although cruelty was endemic in all
slaveholding communities, it was always
most common in newly settled regions.
Along the rough southern frontier thousands
of ambitious men were trying swiftly to
make their fortunes. They operated in a
frantically competitive society which

provided few rewards for the virtues of
gentility and almost put a premium upon
ruthlessness.

In conclusion, Northerners did not have to suffer from a nineteenth century version of existential angst in order for them to be concerned about the perpetuation of slavery. Yet some of Donald's postulates are correct. Just as the Smiths fit his image of Northern abolitionists -- Federalist, educated, middle-class, more agrarian than urban, and religious malcontents -- so also they experienced an increasing sense of displacement. Glastonbury was growing rapidly with cotton mills and mill workers, and power was beginning to shift from the ministers, lawyers, and other professionals to the mill owners and other white males involved in industry. At the beginning of the century, all the Smith women spent long hours every day spinning, weaving, and sewing. Hannah wrote to her mother in 1800 that the daughters had been very busy spinning "and have spun enough for about seventy yards besides almost enough for another carpet." Starting in 1810, Julia's diary is full of notes such as the following on November 21, 1810, "I spun seventeen knots of yarn." But on November 9, 1815, Julia noted that she and Abby had gone to the new cotton mill in town to buy cotton for stockings. From thereon the time they spent spinning and weaving apparently decreased, judging by the drop in diary notations on these subjects.

The ideals so vaunted in the Revolution of an agrarian culture made up of independent, clear-thinking yeoman were already in eclipse by the early nineteenth century, much to the dismay of Federalists such as the Smiths. This sentiment was succinctly expressed by John Adams writing to Thomas Jefferson. "Let me ask you, very seriously my Friend, Where are now in 1813, the Perfection and perfectability [sic] of human Nature? Where is now the progress of the human Mind? Where is the Amelioration of Society? Where the augmentations of human Comforts? Where the diminutions of human Pains and Miseries... When? Where? and how? is the present Chaos to be arranged into Order?"

Having come to adulthood during the heady days of the Revolution when independence was both a national preoccupation and a personal prerogative, Hannah shared the sense of disillusionment which Adams expressed. "October 11, 1849. Sixty years ago, 1783, I wrote I was contented & had been all day, which is so uncommon a thing in the course of one's life that I think it worth noticing. To be in a state of contentment throughout one whole day is rare." Hannah also expressed dissatisfaction, indeed outright contempt, for most politicians, feeling that they had betrayed the ideals of freedom on which the country had been founded. The arguments that the Smiths put forth in the 1830's in opposition to slavery and in the 1870's in support of women's suffrage were based on their understanding of the United States Constitution and the Bill of Rights, documents which they held in highest esteem.

Although such sentiment was indeed the fertile ground in which abolition could grow, it was not the actual seed. At this point what is needed is not supposition but concrete evidence of the Smiths' involvement with people of African descent. On July 4, 1819, a day on which citizens all across the nation were celebrating the achievement of freedom by thirteen colonies which had felt the sting of subjugation to the crown, Julia noted in her diary for the first time that she and her sisters were teaching a Sunday School for black men and women at the First Congregational Church. "I stayed at church and Sunday School. I taught the Negroes." As is frustrating about her entire diary, Julia did not mention how this important event came about or why. All that exists is the flat, unadorned fact. Thus begins many similar entries spanning years:

> I got up a little after the sun. I prepared the
> dinner etc. Zephine and Cyrinthia went this
> morning to Eastbury to see the poor and to
> carry provisions for the sick. We have,
> Laurilla and I, cut out covers for two
> parasols from the green silk I bought
> yesterday. It is hot. I have been with Abby
> this afternoon to Mr. Plummer's to the
> Society. There were fourteen women and
> girls there. We made dresses for the poor
> negresses so they may go to school next
> Sunday.

The following Sunday she arose early so as to read her
Bible quietly before the bustle of the day began. By eight
o'clock she was on her way up Main Street with Mrs. Hale
to the white steepled church, similar in style to thousands
of other Congregational churches throughout New England,
to teach a Sunday school class attended by "negresses," by
which she apparently meant black female children. That
afternoon, she returned to the church at three o'clock,
again with Mrs. Hale, to teach the twenty-two "scholars."
Julia wrote "The mother of two of the little negresses was
there. She cannot read."

Herein lay the crux of a problem which was perplexing
many whites who considered themselves Christian both
North and South, whether slave-holding or not. One of the
prevailing notions with which the Smiths disagreed was that
God had placed in blacks -- along with an inferior brain,
and an emotional, atavistic heart -- a soul. That meant that
God-fearing whites, much to their discomfiture, felt
compelled to teach blacks about the Bible. But how could
that be done if they could not read? And if they learned

how to read, what other books would they want; as a result, what dangerous thoughts would take shape in their wooly, childish heads? In his book *Deep Like the Rivers, Education in the Slave Quarter Community, 1831-1865*, Thomas L. Webber says:

> Perhaps the most common argument against religious instruction was that it tended to make blacks insubordinate by implying that they were as worthy as whites in the eyes of God. Andrew Moss, who worked as a young slave on the large Georgia plantation of George Hopper, relates that his master saw one of his slaves on his knees, "He say, 'What you prayin' about?' And you say. 'Oh, Master, I'se prayin' to Jesus 'cause I wants to go to Heaven when I dies.' And Marster says, 'You's my Negro. I get you to Heaven. Get up offen your knees.' De white folks what owned slaves thought that when dey go to Heaven de colored folks would be dere to wait on 'em.

Although this attitude was endemic throughout the South, Northerners had their own problems determining how far to extend religious and secular education to people who were black. They were allowed to attend church but were required to sit in their own section usually in the back. They were given communion but only after all the whites had partaken. Yet did that mean there was spiritual inequality as well as physical inequality? Were souls ranked in value according to physical traits? It was a dangerous theological conundrum.

To the Smiths, what began as the teaching of religion to little black girls on Sunday morning led to the realization that blacks needed to learn how to read so that they could obtain an understanding about God on their own. As one of their anti-slavery petitions states "to withhold from them the means of acquiring a knowledge of the scriptures is a gross violation of the principles of the gospel." The "means" they were referring to was education.

The Smiths also frequently hired Negro help for chores around the house and on the farm. Julia wrote on August 24, 1819 "Got up at five o'clock. Cold. Did the family ironing. Betsey, a negress, came over to stay with us a few weeks to help us in the kitchen." Two weeks later on September 8, she wrote "I went with Cyrinthia to take some provisions to Richard a negro who is ill. Father went to Hartford this afternoon. I spun ten knots of worsted and three of wool for some stockings for Betsey." At this early date in the diary, there is a paradoxical mixture of both superiority and equality in these diary entries. Whereas Julia called white people by their last names unless they were intimate friends, the Negroes in her life were always called by their first names which reinforced the perception that they were child-like and subservient. At the same time, Betsey came to work "with" the sisters and Julia is content to make her some stockings.

Not a great deal is known about the Negro families that lived in Glastonbury during this period. Prior to 1800 the majority had been slaves who had served as farm hands and domestic help for prosperous farmers. It is probable that most were born in the North where the number of slaves per owner was generally very small. Some of the men had been manumitted from slavery during the Revolutionary War in return for serving in the army in place of their masters, a practice which was made legal by the Connecticut General Assembly in October 1777. Under that law a slave owner had to apply to the selectmen of his town for approval to manumit his slave. Once granted, the owner was released from liability. Some of the Negro men bought their own freedom, meeting the price set by the town selectmen by paying to their masters half their wages received from serving in the Continental army or by bonding themselves out. By about 1800 all Negro men, women and children had bought or been given their freedom in Glastonbury. According to town records, some Negroes owned land. Others worked as laborers and domestic help, earning wages wherever they could. Only one thing was standard: they were all very poor, often living in houses which were no better than shacks in certain sections of town. They were free, at least in comparison to their Southern brothers and sisters, but it was a freedom constricted by poverty and prejudice to the point of hollowness.

As has been pointed out, Julia always referred to Negroes by their first names and then usually added their race. The following entries are included here in their entirety because they place within a daily context a case which Zephaniah tried:

> Tuesday 26 [November 1822] Arose with the sun. Ironed what I washed yesterday. Mother and Cyrinthia went in the carriage to Fortune, the negro's, and afterwards I went out in the carriage with Cyrinthia to see Dimmis. She feels better. I washed the privy, washed the windows of it, etc. Peeled and cut up apples for pies. Cyrinthia made a lot of pumpkin pies. I made two tarts. We bought some beef of Mr. G. Hale and a turkey of Mr. Barnes. I mended one of Father's shirts this evening. Mr. Welles and Samuel Hollister came over tonight. The wife of Ashley Potter has had a child by

Bill, the negro, and they wanted to have him arrested.

Wednesday 27 Arose with the sun. Sewed almost all day on my corset and all evening. Finished it.

Thursday 23 Thanksgiving Day. Got up at seven. Cloudy. I read. It began raining at eleven o'clock. We had dinner at three. It is raining this evening.

Friday 29 Arose at six-thirty. We had breakfast so early we had a candle to see to eat. They arrested the negro and Father is going to Mr. Blinn's [a Glastonbury judge] to pass sentence on him. Fair weather this morning. I sewed on a nightcap. Spun twelve knots of wool this afternoon for a pair of stockings. Mrs. P. Hale and Caroline and Cordelia Hale spent the evening here. They have sent Bill to prison. I began knitting my wool stocking.

Unfortunately, there is no other mention in the diary of Bill, nor any hint of how Julia and her family viewed the affair. All that can be deduced from this entry and the numerous references to the hiring of Negroes is that the Smiths saw them as subordinates. But there is also expressed a personal concern for the welfare of the Negroes living in the community and an awareness that the conditions under which they lived were extremely hard as the next entry makes clear. "Friday 4 [1822] Got up before eight. Cloudy and very cold. I braided more than a yard. Read. This evening I went with Laurilla to take a bed

coverlet to a negro family that is almost without clothes."
Two days later on January 6 Julia went to see "a poor
negro girl who is sick, named Phillis." The next day
Laurilla went to visit her and took her some provisions.
The same week a group of women brought cloth to the
Smith home "to make into clothes for the negroes. My
sisters and I sewed with them. We finished around two
o'clock and Laurilla and I went with three others to put the
clothes on the negroes." Over the next several days the
sisters visited Phillis frequently. On January 24, 1822, Julia
wrote "The cold and wind continue. It is so cold that
Father and Mother do not want us to go see the sick
negress but I hope we can go this evening." But all their
ministrations were for nothing for on February 2, 1822 she
wrote "The poor negro girl died last night. She was alone
when she died. Sister Laurilla went over. She has made a
bonnet for her."

It is a long leap from charitable concern for poor
blacks in Glastonbury to a full-blown commitment to
ending slavery. There is nothing in the diaries and letters
to indicate when the Smiths made that commitment.
Independent thinkers who gave deep thought to everything
they did, it is probable that theirs was not a leap but a
steady movement throughout the 1820's. One thing is clear:
by the early 1830's the Smiths were abolitionists who
called for immediate emancipation of slaves and extension
of equality to free Northern blacks. Somewhere in the
process of going out on a snowy winter night to take bed
coverlets to a destitute Negro family in danger of freezing
to death, of sewing by hand a brand new bonnet for a
dying black woman to wear to her grave, of teaching
wiggly, bright-eyed children about the goodness of God --
somewhere the Smiths came to realize that charity was not
enough. There would never be enough bedquilts to hold
back the cold which came from poverty; there would never

be enough hats. Charity did not change an evil system, it just patched it up until the next day. It was time for action.

*"For this, the unjust shall
not rise up in judgment."
Psalm 1:5a*

7

THE ANTI-SLAVERY
PETITIONS

Sometime during the early to mid-1830's the Smiths joined the Hartford County Anti-Slavery Society and occasionally hosted meetings at their home. An old tree stump (legend has it that it was the stump of an elm tree) made an excellent stand from which abolitionists could regale the crowd with stories about the horrible conditions under which slaves lived. Joseph Wright wrote in his journal of one such gathering on Independence Day 1838. While others around town marched in parades and shot off fireworks commemorating the winning of freedom, Joseph and several others listened in a more sober mood to speeches by "Rev. Messrs. Albert Hale, Lyman, Granger, Andrews, and Plumb and Dr. Chapin of Rocky Hill." The day was fair and extremely hot "thermometer at 95" which apparently did not discourage the speakers who were effective enough to convince Joseph to enroll as a member of the Society.

The Smiths also distributed an anti-slavery newspaper called *The Charter Oak*, taking copies to "the factory village" as Julia called the tenements in South Glastonbury. Versed in current events in Europe, the Caribbean, and the entire United States because of their voracious appetite for newspapers, magazines, tracts, and books, the Smiths knew of the emancipation movement in England, the effects of freedom in places such as Antigua, and slave uprisings in the United States such as Nat Turner's rebellion in Virginia. They also entertained abolitionists in their home including members of Prudence Crandall's family (August 1849), Elihu Burritt (June 1836) who was called "the learned blacksmith" and who would become an important force for world peace, and Richard Rust (January 1840) who would become president of Wilberforce University. They were virtually ubiquitous at state and local anti-slavery meetings and conventions. Furthermore, they crossed the color line. One winter just before Christmas 1842, Julia traveled to Hartford in order to attend "the fair of the people of color." At another time Jehiel Beman, a black minister and underground railroader from Middletown, who had helped form one of the first anti-slavery societies in the state, stopped by to tell Hannah and her daughters about an upcoming convention. Although white abolitionists obviously found slavery onerous, many felt blacks were inferior and kept their distance from them even within the movement; this was not true of the Smiths.

The major source for information on the Smiths' abolition activities are undated drafts of their anti-slavery petitions, resolutions, and letters. The oldest may be as early as the 1820s since a great many anti-slavery petitions were sent to Washington during this period. The size of that particular petition drive, however, was minuscule compared to the two million signatures which overwhelmed Congress ten years later in 1838-39.

The following undated petition draft was definitely written after 1838 because the quote attributed to President Wayland, president of Brown University in Rhode Island, came from a book called *The Limitations of Human Responsibility* published in Boston in 1838:

> President Wayland says "Granting all that may be said of the moral evil of this institution [slavery], granting it to be a violation of the law under which God has constituted moral beings, the question still remains to be decided what is our duty with respect to it." Our duty is to do all in our power as moral beings to abolish such as was scarcely practiced in the barbarian ages, a system of adultery and fornication, most degrading and of the most brutal outrage, parting families and selling them like cattle. It is our duty to assemble as the Constitution allows us and discuss the subject not only to express our disapprobation of the corrupt American slavery system and to advise with regard to the best method of reaching the slave holders' conscience, [crossed out -- and if he has no conscience] to exhort and rebuke, to warn him [crossed out -- them] of the dreadful consequences that the barbarous course he is pursuing will not fail to bring upon them.

President Wayland speaks much of the power not delegated to the citizens of the United States to abolish slavery, but we claim no power save that guaranteed us by the Constitution that the power of speech, the liberty of the press, peaceably to assemble, express our abhorrence of the heinousness of the sin of American slavery.

In 1839 Hannah and all of her daughters undertook to get at least two petitions signed in Glastonbury, apparently visiting almost every house as well as going to the textile mills in South Glastonbury to get signatures from the mill workers. On April 27, 1839 Julia wrote:

This afternoon I have been in the gig with Laurilla as far as the house of Mr. Jones (after having been to the house of Mrs. Norton and M. Jones) to present him with our petition to the legislature on slavery. We returned home at sunset. It is hot and dry. They have put the article of my mother's in the Gazette in reply to Mr. Bushnell.

Later in the same year, a second petition was written and distributed. Julia noted how many signatures they had obtained:

Saturday September 22 -- ...My mother went in the carriage with the minister to bring Zephina to Mr. Jones, the minister to collect some signatures for the petitions for abolition of slavery in the District of Columbia...Zephina came back at night with sixty names.

A few days later the number had risen to 82. When it was finally completed, there were about 400 names. On November 26, Julia wrote "I have written a note to Mr. Trumbull and I have wrapped it up with the petition and this afternoon I walked to the post office and put it in the mail." Unfortunately there is no indication in the Congressional Record that Trumbull actually presented the petition to the United States Congress. However, he did present a petition on February 5, 1840 from residents of South Glastonbury, a section of Glastonbury in which the mills were located, on woolen tariffs. Local lore has it that the Smith petition was presented by John Quincy Adams in January 1840. This is not unlikely since Adams presented hundreds of anti-slavery petitions, whether or not they came from his district. The following petition may have been the one which Julia Smith sent:

> We the undersigned inhabitants of Glastonbury believe that the holding of persons in involuntary slavery [whatever their complex -- scratched out in pen] and regarding them as property is a heinous sin in the sight of their creator. And that to compel them to labor without wages or to withhold from them the means of acquiring a knowledge of the scriptures is a gross violation of the principles of the gospel. And we believe that the selling of human beings as beasts of burden far from their friends and relatives is a cruel practice worthy [of] the barbarous ages whence it originated and deserves the reprehension of all civilized and enlightened people.

Of linguistic significance is the use of the word

"persons," instead of the words "Negroes" or "Africans," and the use of the word "involuntary." In essence, the Smiths were saying that to be held as a slave was against the will of a whole human being -- not a creature who was three-fifth man or woman and two-fifth beast of burden. This is important because most white people, including many white abolitionists, did not consider Negroes as "persons," that is, completely human. They were thought to be a "sub-race," inferior to the white race. In fact, this was the argument slaveholders frequently used in defense of slavery. They contended that black people had to be "kept" because they would never be able to "keep" themselves. From this viewpoint, slavery was not an outrage but a societal necessity. The language which the Smiths chose for the petition implies that they did not believe in racial inferiority. Negroes were full human beings created by God, with the right to choose their way of life, and the ability to study scripture. Inversely, the language used to describe slaveholders placed them outside the pale of civilization, even beyond the mercy of God. In short, slaveholders were uncivilized and unenlightened barbarians.

Heightened rhetoric was often employed by abolitionists, especially by those who were supporters of William Lloyd Garrison. The Smiths believed, as did Garrison, that immediate freedom of slaves would not imperil the safety and economic well-being of the nation, as opponents contended. In fact, on the same page as the draft of the petition, one of the Smiths wrote that slaveholders:

> can give immediate freedom to their slaves
> with perfect safety as exemplified in the
> conduct of the freedmen of Bermuda &
> Antigua (where it has been proved to be for

the interests of both masters & slaves.) That
it is our duty to obtain & to give
information concerning the true state of the
slave and the oppressed people of color of
our land in this land of boasted liberty.

During this period, there were three broad groups of
people concerned with the plight of Negroes: the
immediatists who wanted immediate emancipation, the
gradualists who believed that Negroes should be freed
slowly so as to lessen the negative economic and social
impact on white citizens, and the colonists who believed
that all free Negroes, whether free for generations or
recently manumitted, should be sent back to Africa whether
they wanted to go or not. This last movement had
widespread support until the late 1830's, especially in
Connecticut. Its proponents believed that it offered a
solution to the problem of what should be done with Negro
men and women once they were freed. While many
Northern whites were appalled by the way Negro men and
women were treated as slaves, their sympathy did not
include the idea of equality. Furthermore, they were afraid
that the black race would taint the white race if the two
were allowed to live side-by-side. This is the reason there
was sizable white support for sending blacks back to Africa
where they would not be able to sully the purity of a totally
white United States. As succinctly put by Thomas Jefferson
writing to Governor James Monroe on November 24, 1801,
the entire continent was to be populated "with a people
speaking the same language, governed in similar forms,
and by similar laws; nor can we contemplate with
satisfaction either blot or mixture on the surface."

Free blacks, especially in the North, were appalled by
the prospect of returning to Africa. Many had been in the
United States for generations, predating the arrival of their

white neighbors. They also feared that the removal of free blacks would decrease the pressure on white southerners to end slavery since the value of slaves would increase. They perceived that the African Colonization Movement was really a way to siphon off potential free black leadership, thereby decreasing any chances of revolt or reform, and increasing the power of the slaveowners. Amos Beman, a black man who knew the Smiths personally, wrote from his home in Middletown, "Why should we leave this land so dearly bought by the blood, groans, and tears of our fathers? Truly, this is our home, here let us live, and here let us die."

Approaching the subject of slavery from every conceivable angle, the Smiths also wrote a letter or resolution (rough draft extant) regarding the cessation of foreign slave trade which was supposed to have been banned in 1806. However, as the resolution made clear, slaves had continued to enter the country via Cuba. The Smiths felt that not enough was being done to halt the importation of slaves:

> We must suppose the government of the United States is sincerely disposed to suppress the foreign Slave Trade. Its late measure of sending a ship to the coast of Africa to guard against it evinces the intention of doing something to prevent it. We think Virginia, Kentucky, Tennessee and perhaps some other Slave holding states would also be glad to see a a finalaton [sic] put to it but it will require a great expense to keep a line of guard ships around the coast of Florida to prevent the smuggling of slaves from Cuba.

In all the petitions and resolutions written by the Smiths, there is evidence of the lawyer's careful turn of phrase. Julia had studied the law text "Blackstone" which held the penultimate place of honor in the family library next to the Bible. It is possible the other sisters also studied some law under their father. The first line of the preceding petition is sarcastic; it doesn't state that the Federal government is trying to stop the slave trade as it is committed to do by law; instead it reads "We must suppose the government...is sincerely disposed to suppress the foreign Slave Trade."

There is no date on the above petition or resolution, nor is there any name indicating to whom it was sent. It may have been prompted by the Amistad case which would put it in the 1839-41 period. Julia noted in her diary that the sisters went to see the Negroes of the Amistad who were held first in New Haven and then in Farmington, Connecticut. The case was of enormous interest to all Connecticut abolitionists who suddenly found themselves in the center of a legal controversy which galvanized national interest and clarified some of the pivotal constitutional issues concerning slavery. Owned by Spain, the ship named the Amistad was on its way to Cuba where the Africans on board were to be sold as slaves. Under the leadership of a black man named Cinque, they broke free and killed all but two of the Cuban crew who were kept alive to sail the ship back to Africa. Instead, the Cubans steered east by day but north by night until on August 26, 1839, the ship was seized by Federal authorities off the coast of Long Island. The ship and its passengers was brought into New London, Connecticut. Almost immediately prominent abolitionists began to raise funds for their defense. The ensuing legal battle pitted Spain and the United States, which contended that the Africans were property and therefore should be returned to Spain, against lawyers hired by abolitionists, including Roger Sherman Baldwin, and at the Supreme Court level, John Quincy Adams. Winning their case, the Africans sailed from New York for Sierra Leone in November 1841 but not before many Northerners had come to realize they were intelligent people capable of rational eloquence in their own defense. Of the Mende tribe, the Africans proved to many whites that black people were not three-fifth human, they were five-fifth human.

Clearly, the Smiths were opposed to colonization. In this respect they again followed the lead of William Lloyd Garrison who had been fighting the colonization movement since the first issue of his anti-slavery newspaper *The Liberator* in 1831 and his famous pamphlet *Thoughts on African Colonization* published in 1832. On February 11, 1845, Hannah noted in her diary "A man has been here for us to give to colonization he has gone round with Dea. [deacon] Hale for that end, we gave nothing at all, told him we were abolitionists."

Worthy of note in the Smith petition and addendum is the fact that the Smiths went further than simply advocating the immediate end of slavery. They mentioned specifically the "oppressed people of color" as a separate category, meaning the free black people who were struggling to survive in the face of overwhelming white prejudice. Once again, this was an idea espoused by William Lloyd Garrison who believed that emancipation of blacks was but the first step toward universal emancipation and the end of all kinds of oppression. In fact, in the December 15, 1838 issue of *The Liberator*, Garrison wrote:

> Up to this time, we have limited its [universal emancipation] application to those who are held in this country...as marketable commodities...Henceforth, we shall use it in its widest latitude: the emancipation of our

whole race from the dominion of man, from the thralldom of self from the government of brute force, from the bondage of sin..Next to the overthrow of slavery, the cause of PEACE will command our attention.

In that strong statement Garrison helped lay the groundwork for several other social causes including women's rights and universal suffrage, causes in which the Smiths were also deeply interested. It was impossible for the Smiths and other women abolitionists to theorize about the nature of freedom for women and men who were black without applying their insights to their own constricted lives.

*"The sinful in the assembly
of the just."
Psalm 1:5b*

8

THE PROBLEM OF POLITICAL POWERLESSNESS

As was evident in one of the undated petitions, the Constitutional right to free speech concerned the Smiths deeply and personally. "We claim no power save that guaranteed us by the Constitution, that is the power of speech, the liberty of the press, to petition, and peaceably to assemble, and to express our abhorrence of the heinousness of the sin of American slavery." The inclusion of this list was not a mere formality, underscoring the Smiths' allegiance to the Bill of Rights; it was included because Congress had instituted an anti-petition measure in 1836 in an attempt to stem the tidal wave of anti-slavery petitions. Ardently supported by Southern Congressmen, the gag rule, as it came to be called, prohibited the House of Representatives from printing, discussing, or even mentioning the contents of anti-slavery petitions. Petitions could be "laid on the table" only.

While the gag rule may have stopped the petitions from being discussed, it did not stop them from coming by the thousands. In 1837-38, Congress received over 130,000 petitions calling for the abolition of slavery in the District of Columbia, 32,000 petitions calling for the repeal of the gag rule, 22,000 against the admission of new slave states, 21,000 for legislation barring slavery from western territories, and 23,000 for the abolition of the interstate slave trade.

All of these petitions would have had little significance were it not for John Quincy Adams, former President of the United States and Congressman from Massachusetts, who refused to obey the gag rule. For eight years while the gag rule was in effect, he attempted to read aloud every petition he received, for which he was physically threatened and tried for censure by the House which considered him "the madman from Massachusetts." Since petitions were the only way disenfranchised people had of getting their grievances redressed, Adams was resolutely opposed to stopping them even though they threatened to bury the capitol. He equated the loss of the right of petition with the loss of "every principle of liberty."

The gag rule must have been especially galling to Hannah Smith and her daughters after Zephaniah's death. Since there were no brothers, sons or close male relatives, the rule meant that the Smith women were totally cut off from the political process. One of the predominant reasons given for not allowing women to vote during this period was that they were already represented through their male relatives. With the Smiths, as with thousands of widowed and single women without families, this reason did not hold. But the men in power chose to ignore this group of women since to acknowledge them was to acknowledge the fact that a large group of people were living in a democracy who were subject to its laws (including the payment of taxes), yet had no power whatsoever in their making -- an anomaly that undercut the whole.

Although the right to petition may have paled beside the right to vote, it became all the more important to the Smiths since it was all they had. Whereas for Congressmen the gag rule was a mere convenience which kept the House from being overwhelmed with what it interpreted as nuisance petitions, for the Smiths it was a major attack on their most fragile civil rights. Likewise, the right to free speech which is named in the petition was essential to the Smith women, yet it was routinely denied to them and to all women. Even within the abolition movement itself, there was deep disagreement as to whether women should be allowed to speak publicly. Many female abolitionists, including the Grimke sisters, were roundly condemned for speaking before "promiscuous groups," that is, groups of both men and women, and even Sarah Grimke gave up public speaking after her marriage to Theodore D. Weld. If the Smith women were denied both the right to petition and the right to freedom of speech, then they were denied even the semblance of citizenship.

The furor over the gag rule is an example of a secondary cause being elevated to a primary cause because the secondary cause is either more clear-cut and/or more tolerable to the majority of citizens. The primary cause was abolition of slavery, but that issue had the ability to tear the United States into bloody pieces. In attempting to silence people calling for abolition, southern politicians pushed through the gag rule, thereby depriving citizens of the fundamental right to petition their government. Although many northerners were appalled by slavery, most were not yet ready to risk open conflict. By protesting the deprivation of liberty caused by the gag rule, they were supporting a tangential, politically acceptable (from a northern point of view), socially correct cause. So also the primary cause of the Civil War would be slavery but the secondary cause which would be trumpeted by the South would be state's rights, but of course the "right" of overriding importance was the right to own slaves without interference from the Federal government. From the 1820s to the outbreak of the Civil War, it is hard to find a national political issue around which the dreaded specter of slavery did not float.

There are several entries in Hannah's diary expressing her dismay with certain pieces of proposed legislation and her disgust with politicians in general, with the primary issue always being slavery. Hannah even used poetry to convey her feelings about abolition and its opponents. There is a rough draft of a poem called "Slaveholders in Congress Speaking of Northern Doughfaces." In part it reads:

And how we shame them -- Abolition
Is a word they will disclaim
As if it would be their perdition
To be suspect of the name, must
thus they begin -- "I insist
I am no Abolitionist."

Hannah was deeply opposed to President James K. Polk's invasion of Mexico in 1846 and expressed her views in strong language in her diary as well as in numerous letters to many congressmen, whom she categorized on December 3, 1846 as a "furious long number of the rascals, upholding war & slavery."

I shall not try to enumerate all the vagaries of our government with Polk as its head, last year and this. Its spirit of aggrandizement, not to say robbery, that plung'd us into a war unjust & unnecessary with Mexico, was most outrageous to all the feelings of humanity; as unprovoked aggression on that country & persisted in contrary to all the customary usages of civilized nations, a stain on our country which not all the gold of California, were it a blessing, instead of a curse, could wash out or even obliterate in the view of foreign countries when they estimate the national character of the Americans. It was a most unprecedented act of invasion on an independent Republic.

Abolitionists saw Polk's land hunger as a thinly disguised conspiracy by southern politicians, beginning with Andrew Jackson, to increase slaveholding land, an increase made necessary by the impoverishment of the soil in the deep south caused by cotton. John Quincy Adams was vehemently opposed to the annexation of Mexico. Never forgetting that his defeat at the hands of Andrew Jackson in 1828 was largely due to southern slaveholders, Adams denounced annexation as theft of free soil from Mexico in order to bring in new slave states which would then dominate the Union. So deep was his commitment that he collapsed and died at his desk in 1848 while preparing to speak out one more time against Polk's expansionism.

It followed, therefore, that Hannah was also dismayed by the reception that the Wilmot Proviso received in the Senate. First proposed in 1846 by David Wilmot, Democratic congressman from Pennsylvania, the Proviso would have barred slavery in the territories to be purchased from Mexico. Although it passed the House in 1846 and 1847, Southern senators led by John C. Calhoun defeated the measure both times. On February 19, 1847, Hannah noted: "The Wilmot bill against slavery in California has passed the House. I doubt if it does the Senate. A part of Calhoun's speech is an outrage against civilization."

As the 1840's progressed, the problem over extension of slavery into the newly opened western territories grew larger and more intractable. Many Northerners found slavery morally objectionable, but their feelings were not strong enough to motivate them to take time out of their daily lives to distribute petitions, write their Congressmen, or shelter runaway slaves. As long as the "evil" stayed put in the southern states, it could be ignored to a degree. It was even possible for some northerners to still harbor the illusion that it was withering away. The fight for the extension of slavery into the west totally shattered that illusion, forcing moderates off the fence and into the political arena. The anger and frustration which grew in the north was expressed sardonically by Hannah in November 1844 (no day given in diary). "It has been a great day with politicians, ten yoke of oxen have gone by with a cart full and a flag with Polk & Dallas on it. I cannot blame the oxen, they do not know any better."

Politically speaking, the Smiths had no more rights than the ten yoke of oxen laboring to pull the cart loaded down with office seekers and party supporters. Forced to rely on letters and petitions, which coming as they did from non-voting women could be totally ignored by politicians, the Smiths may have resorted to more clandestine means of achieving their ends. There have always been persistent rumors that the Smiths were part of the underground railroad during the 1840's and 1850's, partially because it seemed a logical extension of their abolitionism. However, their letters and diaries cannot be used to prove or disprove that rumor. Members of the underground railroad tended to be very circumspect about writing down their activities. The only evidence may be circumstantial. Who visited the Smiths? How often did they travel to certain locations such as Middlefield or Farmington, Connecticut, which were known stops on the underground railroad?

The underground railroad, long active in the border states, picked up steam in Connecticut following the passage of the Fugitive Slave Act which was part of the Compromise of 1850. Under this act any person who was caught aiding a fugitive slave was subject to six months imprisonment and $2,000 in damages and fines. A U.S. marshall could be fined $1,000 for refusing to arrest and detain a fugitive slave. No matter how long men and women had been free, they could be extradited to the state or territory from which they had escaped with the only proof of ownership required by law being the oath of the slaveholder. This particular piece of legislation was too much for even lukewarm white Northerners to stomach. Many people did not have the interest or the backbone to be active abolitionists, but neither were they about to let slaveowners walk into New England and demand that the citizenry help them reclaim what they said was theirs without written proof. The result was that many white Connecticut citizens who found slavery morally onerous, even though it was legal under Federal law, chose to close their eyes to the presence, albeit brief, in their towns of runaway slaves heading to Canada via Connecticut. That didn't mean the majority of white citizens helped Negroes in their exodus; it only meant they chose not to impede their flight north. Simultaneously, free blacks who had lived in Connecticut for years felt deeply threatened by the Fugitive Slave Act, fearing that they would be mistaken for runaway slaves and dragged south. As a result, many men and women decided to head north, causing a steep decline in the Negro population in the state. Of those who chose to remain, some became conductors on the underground railroad.

One of the Negro families which took an active role in the underground railroad in Connecticut was the Bemans. Jehiel Beman, a minister in Middletown, and his son Amos Gerry Beman, a minister in New Haven, openly boasted of their involvement. On January 13, 1851, Amos Gerry Beman wrote to Rev. S.R. Ward "On the sixth instant, we had the privilege of receiving and sending on her way an interesting passenger from the land of chains + whips by the underground railroad...Who will blot out the North Star?" Of significance in terms of the Smiths' involvement is an entry in Hannah's diary for November 12, 1849 "Mr. Beman, colored man, call'd to bring a pamphlet about their convention." Obviously, Hannah knew Jehiel Beman. In fact, he had spoken at the Methodist Meeting House in South Glastonbury, only about two miles from the Smith home, several years earlier on January 8, 1838, at which time an anti-slavery society was formed. There is no record that the Smiths attended. They were already members of the Hartford County Anti-Slavery Society. However, given the depth of their commitment, their presence at that meeting would have been likely.

The main underground railroad route in Connecticut ran from New Haven up the Connecticut river valley often along the western side via Middlefield and Farmington up to Springfield, Massachusetts, but there were also less traveled routes on the eastern side of the river which ran from Portland through Glastonbury up to Bolton and from there north into Massachusetts. Although there is nothing definite about the involvement of the Smiths with the underground railroad, there are some cryptic references in

Hannah's diaries which may refer to the underground railroad. For example, on February 19, 1847 she wrote "Julia has been to Mr. Kibain this evening to inform them of what they did not know and Laurilla has gone to Capt. Turner on the same account." There are several other cryptic entries including this one from September 9, 1844 "Just about dark Mr. Beckwith brought a man woman & two children here today all night & two horses to be kept on hay, he is Rusty Wire, inte... [illegible]." Then there is the following entry for June 20, 1845 "Last night Emily was here [illegible] a stranger to talk, would not tell his name." Emily Moseley was the very close friend of the family who met with the sisters weekly during the 1840's and 50's to review Julia's translation of the Bible.

One must proceed cautiously, however, in making the assumption that the Smiths were part of the underground railroad based upon a few veiled comments in their diaries. Consideration must be given to another dairy entry dated December 22, 1848 "Last night Dea (deacon) & negro came for assistance to go to Canada. Our folks gave him a dollar." The question must be asked why Hannah would veil entries about helping runaway slaves and then be so open about helping this one on his way to Canada. In conclusion, nothing can be said with certainty about the Smith's involvement in the underground railroad. It cannot be assumed that simply because they were ardent abolitionists they were likewise underground railroaders. Most abolitionists were not; there was a great difference between espousing a cause, no matter how vehemently, and actually breaking the law and risking life and limb to see that cause triumph.

In her diary, Hannah revealed both her continued interest in abolition and her increasing weariness. The following entry was written on July 4, 1849, when she was almost 82 years old.

> It is a day kept in various ways thro' the
> whole United States. It has been celebrated
> here under our shades several times by the
> young and by the old, the last time since
> Mr. Smith's death it was kept by a company
> of Abolitionists, about ten or a dozen
> ministers with them to make speeches, sing,
> etc. but I was always so much fatigued that
> I never saw any pleasure in it. I am thankful
> we are now too considerate to take part in
> companies where there is so much bustle
> and confusion and so little satisfaction, or
> rather none at all, even at the best.

On December 27, 1849, Hannah wrote in her diary
"Abby unwell. I have been in her room reading Josephus."
Soon she became seriously ill herself and although both
were to recover, Hannah never regained her health
completely. She died the next year on December 27, 1850
at age 83, on a day of sustained cold when "the sun
produces no effect on the snow." Her death left a deep
spiritual hole in the family that would never be filled. In
writing to a friend of the family in 1854, Julia said "of her
much lamented mother" that "in letter writing I have
seldom seen her equal, and so accustomed was she to use
her pen that in her last painful sickness she called for her
journal and wrote though unable to sit up."

Laurilla died seven years later in March 1857, a
windy, chilly month. Among her daily reports of weather
in her small meteorological folio, Julia inserted:

> 19th March 1857. Let.[sic] Smith died at
> half past eleven. Mrs. Porter and Mrs.
> Turner came to help lay her out. More than
> twenty-two persons called. Abby quite sick.

Using pen and ink, Laurilla Smith sketched the home of George Talcott in 1828. The two paintings entitled *Tippoo Saib Delivering His Sons to the English* were painted in watercolor on silk. They are in the collection of the Connecticut Historical Society in Hartford.

Hannah and Zephaniah Smith purchased their home from Anna Kimberly Brace and her husband in 1795. It was located on a narrow piece of land which stretched for three miles from the Connecticut River to the wooded uplands. As painted by Laurilla Smith in watercolor, the Smith homestead was a center-chimney farmhouse with shutters, a lean-to addition on the back, outbuildings, grape arbors, and picket fences. (The Connecticut Historical Society, Hartford, Connecticut.)

Refused the right to address the electors on April 6, 1874, Abby Smith, age 76, mounted a wagon outside the town hall and spoke to the crowd. Using the analogy of siblings who have equal property rights, she charged that if the brothers made a law depriving the sisters of their share, the sisters would not be bound by it. So also women should not be bound by laws made by men. The town hall portrayed in this 1893 photograph is now the home of the Historical Society of Glastonbury.

This is the only extant photo of Julia and
Abby Smith. It was taken during their
famous battle with the Town of
Glastonbury over the issue of taxation
without representation.

The etching entitled "Abby Smith and Her Cows" appeared
as the frontispiece in the chapbook by the same name
published by Julia Smith in 1877 to publicize and raise
money for their tax battle.

HOUSEHOLD GOODS

AT

AUCTION

ON

WEDNESDAY, APR. 23

AT THE

Smith Sisters' Mansion House

GLASTONBURY.

The only survivor of the family, Julia E. Smith Parker, having sold the Homestead Farm and about to remove from the place will sell at auction a large lot of Household Furniture, being the accumulation of almost a century and too numerous and various to be particularly mentioned.

Among which may be mentioned: a London made Piano, a large Looking Glass, an antique Case of Drawers, large and small brass Scuttles, brass Andirons, Shovel and Tongs, Iron Ware, Tin Ware, Wooden Ware, Tables, Sofas, Chairs, five Spinning Wheels, Baskets, 8 or 10 cords of fire-wood seasoned in wood-house, good family two seated covered Carriage about as good as new, also, about 50 Bibles translated from the original languages by herself and published at her expense.

Sale to commence at 10 A. M. and continue until all are sold.

Glastonbury, Conn., April 9, 1884.   JULIA E. SMITH PARKER.

Friends of the Smiths were aghast when the Smith household goods were auctioned off after Abby's death and Julia's ill-advised marriage to Judge Amos Parker.

JULIA E SMITH

BORN

MAY 27, 1792.

DIED

MARCH 6, 1886.

Apparently realizing her error in marrying Amos Parker, Julia Smith left a note in her Bible a few years before her death asking that she be buried in Glastonbury with the rest of her family and that her maiden name, not her married name, appear on the gravestone. (Photo by Duffy.)

Together in death as in life, the Smith graves are located in the cemetery next to the Glastonbury town hall which was the site of Julia's and Abby's vehement protests about taxation and suffrage. (Photo by Duffy.)

In 1832 Erastus Salisbury Field, an itinerant portrait
painter, came to Glastonbury and painted pictures of the
entire Smith family. All have been lost except that of
Zephaniah. (The Museum of Fine Arts, Springfield,
Massachusetts, Given in Memory of Holger Cahill.)

Such a sudden death has overwhelmed the whole family. Mr. Talcott has brought the coffin from Hartford and has the care of the funeral. A Morton stayed here all afternoon.

Ever the one in control, Julia wrote two days later:

All slept below. Had a real weep this morning. C. and A. so unwell they cannot go to the funeral. I made three fires, one in Abby's chamber. I moved C. and A. up there. Mrs. Porter and Mrs. Talcott and Helen Turner came to arrange the corps [sic] and Mr. Porter and Henry Talcott to put it in the coffin. Priscilla came this morning and stayed until the funeral which was held at 3 o'clock...Mr. Talcott carried her unto the grave. Oh, can we bear to live without such a dear sister.

From here on a sister would die every seven years. As a reporter for *The Sunday Republican* wrote "Once in every seven years the black-winged messenger visited the homestead and called away one of its household until he had gathered them all on the other side of the dark river. Had they, perhaps, in their long and busy lives found nothing certain but death and taxes?" Yet, though down in numbers and in spirit, the remaining sisters would fill their last years with as much activism as the prior fifty, with Abby being the most outspoken.

During the Civil War, the sisters were deeply suspicious of Lincoln's motives as regards both the war and emancipation. Although Lincoln was opposed to slavery, he was not for immediate abolition, supporting instead a gradualist approach. When he was elected President, he hoped to hold the Union together and to contain the spread of slavery, not bring about its immediate end. Even after his Emancipation Proclamation, he was uncertain about its constitutionality. Many abolitionists were infuriated by Lincoln's attitude. Having supported him initially, they felt betrayed and began to criticize him unmercilessly. Exactly this attitude is revealed in a letter which Abby wrote to Mrs. Charlotte Gillett, dated Sept. 21, 1862:

> What can we or anybody think of this horrible war. It seems to us precisely as it seems to you, respecting [illegible] and generals at headquarters. I cannot bear to <u>read</u> about it & you are obliged to <u>see & feel it</u> and we may be. You speak of England, I do not know as we can blame her for favoring the South which is most to her advantage if both parties intend to keep slavery. You know our government at W. has always declared both in word & action that it was not a war for emancipation and appears to watch over the wicked institution as tenderly as the South, notw- [notwithstanding] they know & everybody knows that it is the cause of the war. If we will not put down the cause of the war how must we conquer without?

Abby was also dissatisfied with the behavior of other abolitionists and members of Lincoln's cabinet. In a letter to Charles C. Burleigh on September 9, 1862, she charged that abolitionists in the area had all joined the Republicans and compromised slavery in their zeal for the party. "We (myself & sisters) have stood alone." Although she and her sisters had wanted to see Lincoln elected (though lacking the vote, they could do nothing to bring it about), they had lost confidence from the moment he had delivered his first inaugural address in which he had promised to "preserve, protect and defend" the Union but not outlaw slavery. They were also concerned because they felt that some members of his cabinet lacked integrity. "I very much fear the country will not be saved."

Though pleased about the Emancipation Proclamation on September 22, 1862, having worked for it for over thirty years, the Smiths' response was understandably subdued. True, slavery had come to an end, but in the midst of a bloody, unending war constantly bungled by Union generals, there was no time for jubilation, for what did an end to slavery mean if the North lost? The Confederacy was bound to uphold it. And even for the northern free states, how meaningful could the Proclamation be when Lincoln himself was ambivalent toward blacks, an ambivalence made manifest, according to Abby, in his slowness to give black soldiers the same pay for the same labor during the War. This antagonism toward Lincoln did not abate even when victory became more certain in early 1865. What would reconstruction be like, Abby wondered, when the administration denied "the black man his rights because he is black after they have defended us & have shown themselves to be the only true friends we have at the South."

On and on the war dragged, with the body count climbing into the hundreds of thousands and no end in sight. It was while William Tecumseh Sherman was laying siege to Atlanta in August 1864 and Ulysses S. Grant was bloodily bogged down outside of Petersburg that Cyrinthia Sacretia died on August 19, 1864 at the age of 76. Her undiagnosed illness was long and debilitating, and in seeking to be healed, she traveled to a hydropathy clinic in New York State to take what was called the "water cure."

This involved wrapping her body in cold wet bandages over which were placed warm dry blankets. It also involved drinking great quantities of water, the intent being to draw out of the body any impurities that were causing the illness. Although Cyrinthia stayed sixteen weeks and three days, the water cure did not help at all, and in fact the other sisters were dismayed by what they considered the poor medical treatment she received. Furthermore, they felt that they were overcharged by one of the doctors because they were women.

Writing about Cyrinthia's death to an abolitionist named Dr. Hudson a year later on July 27, 1865, Abby wrote:

> We have had a sad winter without our sister. She never spent one from home & the sister [Zephina] that had roomed with her all her life could hardly support the loss. It affected her health, but she has been better this spring & is now quite well. Julia and I have been very well but it has been a hard task for us to take care of all the fruit trees, grapes & strawberry vines our late sister had raised and cultivated. We have now excellent sweet apples of her grafting and abundance of another kind that will keep till August. We sent the last of her grapes to invalids this past week about as good as when gathered. We have had plenty all winter.

Although Laurilla had been buried with a funeral, Cyrinthia was buried without benefit of clergy. In a letter dated August 25, 1864, Abby wrote "The 40 chapters of Isaiah beginning at the 6 verse was selected & read by a friend which was the only service performed... And now all is over she rests peacefully in her grave beside our father." How apt was the Book of Isaiah! Chapter 1:6 reads "From the sole of the foot even to the head, there is no soundness in it, but bruises and sores and bleeding wounds; they are not pressed out, or bound up, or softened by oil. Your country lies desolate, your cities are burned with fire" (King James Version). Yet the 40th chapter ends with one of the most exalting pieces of scriptures in the entire Bible. "Even youths shall faint and be weary, and young men shall fall exhausted; but they who wait for the Lord shall renew their strength, they shall mount up with wings like eagles, they shall run and not be weary, they shall walk and not faint."

The three remaining Smiths were not fainting youths or exhausted young men. They were old women who had lost their parents and two beloved sisters. They had fought hard for emancipation and finally won. They had a right to rest on the sidelines, reminiscing about their days of activism. But that was not to be. In the years left to them following the Civil War, they would instead renew their strength and mount up with wings like eagles. They would run and not be weary. They would walk and not faint.

"His leaf shall not
fall away."
          Psalm 1:3

9

RE-SOUNDING THE BATTLE CRY:

TAXATION WITHOUT REPRESENTATION

It is rare that the last few decades of life are the most active. Generally the years beyond the seventieth birthday are filled with remembrance not remonstrance, but for the remaining Smith sisters, this was not to be the case. Abolition had taught them many vital political lessons they were not about to forget, neither had the deaths of Zephaniah, Hannah, Laurilla, and Cyrinthia quenched their fighting spirits. This time, however, it would be Abby who would lead the charge, while Julia, the cerebral writer, would document the entire battle, publishing a chapbook entitled *Abby Smith and Her Cows*, which was comprised principally of favorable press clippings.

During their involvement with abolition, the Smiths' concern about the rights of Negroes worked in conjunction with their awareness that as women they, too, were politically powerless. In fact, social norms dictated that they were not even to hold, let alone voice, an opinion on such an important subject as abolition. If they did have an opinion, the vast majority of males thought they should keep it to themselves. So incensed were the Congregational clergy of Massachusetts at women, such as Sarah and Angelina Grimke, who dared to speak publicly about anti-slavery that they issued the following pastoral letter in 1837:

> When the mild, dependant [sic] influence of woman upon the sternness of man's opinions is fully exercised, society feels the effects of it in a thousand forms. The power of woman is her dependence, flowing from the consciousness of that weakness which God has given her for her protection...But when she assumes the place and tone of man as a public reformer, our care and protection of her seem unnecessary...If the vine, whose strength and beauty is to lean upon the trellis work and half conceal its clusters, thinks to assume the independence and overshadowing nature of the elm, it will not only cease to bear fruit, but fall in shame and dishonor in the dust.

Ironically, many male abolitionists, including clergy, who had been combating claims that slavery was sanctioned by the Bible by approaching the subject allegorically, suddenly interpreted the Bible literally when it came to women's rights. Angelina Grimke countered that there was no such thing as a man's rights or a woman's rights, only human rights, but there were no winners in this scripture-slinging battle. Equally grating to the Smiths was the fact that many women agreed with the men, believing that God had indeed made them to "lean upon the trellis" and not express themselves. On July 25, 1839, Hannah wrote to Abigail Kelley, a dedicated abolitionist, public speaker, and member of the American Anti-Slavery Society, about the difficulty of getting signatures on their petition:

> I am glad to find it is painful to some besides ourselves to witness the apathy that prevails in this state to the cause of antislavery.... Women have been taught to depend on the men for their opinions; we had occasion to observe this, in our efforts to obtain signatures to petitions; my daughters visited almost every house in this town for that purpose & found it was the men, generally, who needed "free discussion," for the women would not act contrary to the ideas of the male part of their families; there was but one exception -- One woman made her son sign her name, tho' the young man was much opposed.

Two years after that letter in 1841, Abby Kelley's name was put forth by William Lloyd Garrison to sit on the board of the American Anti-Slavery Society. Her nomination caused a furor which split the Society down the middle. Those opposed walked out of the national convention and formed their own organization, the American and Foreign Anti-Slavery Association, in which women were not only barred from holding office but from speaking publicly. To Garrisonians, such as the Smiths, not to allow women to speak was to make moot the entire debate about freedom from slavery. The Smith women were fully aware of the irony of working for abolition at the same time that they themselves were denied the right to vote and the right to speak in public.

This denial was made more acute because of the move in many states toward universal white male suffrage which meant that a white male no longer had to own a certain amount of property or attain a certain level of education in order to be allowed to vote. Making matters worse was the influx of European and Irish immigrants into the United States during the antebellum era. Many women's rights activists, such as Elizabeth Cady Stanton, were angered by the extension of the vote to landless, uneducated, foreign-born, male citizens when they themselves were landed, educated, and American-born female citizens.

But the abolition movement had given women much more than awareness of inequity. In her essay "Women's Rights and Abolition: The Nature of the Connection," Ellen DuBois stated that:

> Garrison abolitionism provided women with a political framework that assisted the development of a feminist movement. As Garrisonians, women learned a way to view the world and a theory and practice of social change that they found most useful in elaborating their protofeminist insights. In addition, the antislavery movement provided them with a constituency and a political alliance on which they were able to rely until the Civil War. Thus, American feminism developed within the context of abolitionism less because abolitionists taught

women that they were oppressed than
because abolitionists taught women what to
do with that perception, how to develop it
into a social movement.

This statement holds true for the Smiths who did not
need abolition to teach them about freedom. Although their
withdrawal from activism due to the physical depredations
of advancing age would have been understandable, the
remaining sisters were blessed with an abundance of health
and energy. Picking up where they had left off before the
Emancipation Proclamation, the sisters revamped their
abolitionist ideas in the late 1860's and began to fight for
their own rights. According to Julia, it all began over a
small highway tax of $18.00 which was presented to the
sisters in June 1869. Although the sum was not due until
October, the collector asked that they pay it immediately
since he had wages to pay to the crew repairing the roads
and he "could get no money from the men." The sisters
obliged, only to find to their consternation that they were
rebilled for the same amount in October. When Julia
questioned the tax collector, he began complaining about
the ineptitude of the Democratic officials then in power, he
himself being a Republican. He also complained about a
charge of $700 spent by the town to register men to vote.
Incensed to find that what she considered to be an
inordinate amount of her taxes was spent to register men,
Julia concluded that she "must go to that suffrage meeting
in Hartford and see if we cannot do better, for I have no
doubt one woman would write down every name in town
for half that money."

Two days later on a "raw, sour day" in November,
Julia and Abby traveled the seven miles to Hartford on
snow-covered roads to attend the first convention of the
Connecticut Woman Suffrage Association, which was held

in the Opera House. Organized by John Hooker and his wife Isabella Beecher Hooker, the youngest daughter of Lyman Beecher, the convention was enlivened by speeches of Elizabeth Cady Stanton, Caroline Severence, Susan B. Anthony, William Lloyd Garrison, and Julia Ward Howe. It was a good thing these speeches were heated and impassioned because the Opera House was unheated and the attendees had to rely solely on the pyrotechnics of the speakers as well as their own inner fire for warmth. The Smiths listened to Susan B. Anthony tell in a "candid, kindly and sensible way" about several instances where women were cheated out of fair wages because they did not have the vote. Especially memorable was her account of a petition for higher wages presented to the school board by eight male teachers and one hundred and twenty five female teachers in Rochester, New York. As a result, the men who already received $800 per year were given raises of $100 while the women who received $400 a year if they functioned as principals had their wages decreased by $25. "If those one hundred and twenty-five women had each possessed the ballot, would the board have dared to take that course?" Anthony asked. "We need a power that will give rulers a motive for giving us what we have a right to demand," she concluded.

Resolutions drafted by John Hooker were also put forth calling for suffrage to be extended to women because "the ballot will bring to woman higher education, larger industrial opportunities, a wider field for thought and action, a sense of responsibility in her relations to the public welfare, and in place of mere complaisance and flattery, the higher and truer respect of men." At the end of the long, cold day, the Smiths returned to Glastonbury with a new resolve to work for woman suffrage. "We could stay only one session, and came home believing that the women had truth on their side; but never did it once enter

our heads to refuse to pay taxes." When in the early spring
of 1874, the Smiths delivered their stinging and powerful
suffrage speeches while standing in a farm wagon drawn up
outside the town hall, having been barred from speaking to
the men gathered within, they would be accused by some
male listeners of being hired to cause trouble by the
suffrage conventions they had attended. To this charge,
Abby stoutly replied that prior to attending any convention,
she and her sister had reached their own conclusion that "it
was not right that our money should be taken from us by
force, when men themselves declared that 'governments
derived their just powers from the consent of the
governed.' We had not consented, and therefore, we were
bound by no law to pay taxes."

Although their interest in suffrage was high, it would
be three years before a clear opportunity for action would
present itself and yet another year still before they would
get the chance to voice publicly their stand on taxation
without representation. One reason for the delay was the
death of the eldest sister Hancy Zephina on June 30, 1871
at the age of 84. A mainstay in their lives since the
moment of their births, her death upset Julia and Abby
greatly for they had never been separated from her. They
considered Zephina "the life of the house," and an
individual with a "keen sense of injustice."

A year passed before the two remaining sisters
returned to the issue of taxation and suffrage. In 1872 the
town tax collector, a man by the name of Cornish, called
at the Smiths to collect their taxes. The sisters were
surprised to find that their assessment had increased by
$100. "To be sure it increased our tax but little, but what
is unjust in least is unjust in much." What was especially
galling to Julia and Abby was the fact that the only other
people in town whose assessments had increased were two
widows; not a single man was so affected. The Smiths

protested that because they were elderly women they could not themselves put their land to productive use as could men who raised tobacco for a cash crop. Being among the wealthier families in town, their protestations of inability to pay did not impress the tax collector. Even so, Mr. Cornish left without collecting any money. After consulting with the town selectmen as to how he should handle the situation, he returned several days later with preemptory orders to collect $200. This time the sisters acquiesced and paid that amount, but it apparently angered Abby far more than the highway tax in 1869. Julia commented on Abby's response as follows:

> My sister who has the most courage of the two, and seemed to think almost the whole of our native town friendly to us, declared she was not going to be so unjustly used, without telling of it. I warned her of the consequences, and as we had so short a time to stay here, we had better submit; and asked how she would do it? She said, when the men met in town meeting.

About this time Julia, Abby, a close Glastonbury friend and suffragist named Rosella Buckingham, and two other unnamed women tried to register to vote in Glastonbury and were turned down. The facts as presented in a draft of a letter dated March 29, 1873 but with an addendum written the following month and the newspaper version printed in *Abby Smith and Her Cows* differ somewhat in terms of order of events, but the gist of it was that the registrars insisted the town selectmen had the authority to turn down the women's request, whereas the selectmen insisted the right remained with the registrars. Whether the disagreement was planned in secret or not, the result was to tie up bureaucratically the process of registering to vote so that once their application was turned down, the women would not have the necessary time to appeal. "We feel very ill used," Julia protested. However, Rosella Buckingham had determined that by law their rejection could be appealed to the town selectmen, which the three women did in person in March 1873. The group was meeting in the town hotel. The three women waited patiently in the parlor until called into the room in which the selectmen and the registrars were seated around a square table. One of the selectman who was a lawyer stoutly denied that they had the right to appeal but Rosella persisted. Their initial rejection had been made on the basis that the word "male" had not been expunged from the Constitution and the town did not wish to act contrary to law. Rosella countered that argument by pointing out that the word "white" had not been expunged either yet the laws now pertained to blacks. The town clerk then read the new constitutional amendments and agreed with the women that if "Negro" could come in under state law so also could "women," but the lawyer strongly disagreed. What especially irked the three women was that the "veriest vagabond that walked the streets to whose support we were liable, who never paid the town a dollar, whose poll tax even they had to remit -- this man had been given by the town power which they were not willing to give to us & he could take our property from us. What we were asking the town was to be put on a level with this man. We did not ask for more power than was given to him, we wanted the same law to judge both." But logical argument and strong unemotional demands made no difference. The answer was no. Undaunted, the women attended another meeting about a month later at which they were greeted with cordiality and came away believing that their demands were at least viewed favorably.

Lillian Prudden visited the Smiths more frequently during this period because her "mother had proved herself advanced enough to have me go to college and particularly after my brother Henry courteously escorted Julia and Abby to a large suffrage meeting where he helped them to the seats on the platform to which they were invited." In her memoirs, she wrote about the physical impression they made:

> Julia was short and plain in looks making many little jerks of her head to emphasize her always strong opinions. I remember her coming once with a little box in her hand, saying 'Mrs. Kellogg thinks my hair is getting so thin that I need to cover the top of my head and I thought you would help me put this headdress on.' It was a difficult task to keep it on for the first vehement turn in the conversation sent the cap down over one ear. Her bonnets had the same inclination. She was so supremely indifferent to dress that she had to be watched lest she put on her dress the wrong side out. Abby was tall and much more dignified in carriage and was always carefully and neatly dressed.

Whether dignified or indifferent, the Smiths' presence at town meetings must have made the men awkward and uncertain how to act. Having been born in the eighteenth century, Julia and Abby were old enough to be the greatgrandmothers of some of the selectmen. Their very age demanded that the men at least treat them politely. Furthermore, they were upstanding, wealthy citizens who had been on the right side of the abolition cause when many people in Glastonbury were at best ambivalent. In short, by the 1870s they had taken on the aura of unshakable righteousness. Yet for all the town meetings that the Smiths attended, there is not a single mention in the town records of their presence or their requests. Rosella Buckingham felt that though the men in Glastonbury were benevolent, the interest of the best of the men were not identical with those of the women and as a result they were utterly "unable to assist the ladies in their struggles for the rights of self-government." Uppermost on the selectmen's minds during this period was a boundary dispute with the Town of Wethersfield across the Connecticut River. The Smiths were pesky gadflies, not even worth a penciled-in note. As the moderator of the selectmen's meeting put it, the battle was a "tempest in a teapot."

Not until the following fall when taxes again became due did Abby get a chance to act on her resolve to force the issue of taxation without representation. On October 13, 1873, Abby and Julia traveled south to New York City to attend the convention of the American Woman Suffrage Association. This deepened their conviction that they had to act on their principles and refuse to pay taxes if the town once again denied them the right to vote. And so a month after returning from the convention, on a cold day in November, 1873, Julia and Abby rode down to the red brick town hall next to the graveyard in which all the rest of their family lay buried. The men were gathered inside for the town meeting when Abby and Julia entered. Abby asked for and received permission to speak. A woman "rather above medium height, with a face in which culture and kindness mingle to a marked degree," Abby delivered a well-written, hard-driving speech:

> It is not without due deliberation that we
> have been willing to attend this meeting, but
> we had no other way of coming before the

men of the town. Others, our neighbours, can complain more effectually than we can, without speaking a word, when they think those who rule over them rule with injustice; but we are not put under the laws of the land as they are -- we are wholly in the power of those we have come to address.

Gathering steam, she drew on many of the arguments the Smiths had used during abolition:

People do not generally hold power without exercising it, and those who exercise it do not appear to have the least idea of its injustice. The Southern slaveholder only possessed the same power that you have to rule over us. "Happy dog," he would say of his slave, "I have given him everything; I am the slave, and he the master; does he complain? give him ten lashes." The slaveholders really thought they had done so much for their slaves they would not leave them, when the great consideration was, the slave wanted control of his own earnings; and so does every human being of what rightfully belongs to him.

Abby then argued that men who paid taxes had a say in how those taxes were spent. If their assessments were increased, they had recourse to the ballot box to change the administration which was misusing the money. But women did not have any recourse at all "..from the men of our town we are never safe -- they can come in and take our money from us just when they choose." Stressing that women were created by God with as much intelligence as men, Abby made the point that they should be treated equally:

> The motto of our government is "Proclaim liberty to all the inhabitants of the land," and here where liberty is so highly extolled and gloried by every man in it, one-half the inhabitants are not put under her laws, but are ruled over by the other half, who can by their own laws, not hers, take from the other half all they possess. How is Liberty pleased with such worship? Would she not be apt to think of her own sex?

Without mincing her words, Abby accused the politicians in town of buying votes, even taking men from the insane asylum and keeping "them in a barn to vote the next day." She charged that the town officials dropped the poll tax for poor vagabonds so that they could vote and then entertained themselves at the town's expense. "We have paid the town of Glastonbury during the last six years more than $1000, and for what? to be ruled over and be put under, what all the citizens know to be the lowest and worthless of any in the place?"

This was not a speech designed to win male friends and indeed it did not, for no man present spoke in their defense and by the time the sisters left, nothing had been resolved. As a reporter for the *Boston Daily Advertiser* (January 13, 1874) put it "the address was quietly listened to, and its suggestions were scrupulously ignored." But the sisters were too politically savvy to let the issue lie. They submitted the speech to *The Hartford Courant* which printed it in its entirety. *The Springfield Republican* also printed an article about the speech, saying it "was a very creditable address for a woman who has not devoted herself to public speaking."

No matter how good the speech, it did not deter the new tax collector, a man named George Andrews from calling on the Smiths and demanding payment. (Mr. Cornish, the previous tax collector, had been thrown from a sleigh and killed the winter before.) Once again the sisters refused, telling him as they had told the men at the town meeting that he could begin to take their farm away from them starting at the eastern end, sparing for them the homestead which lay near the western end of the property, just above the meadows which bordered the Connecticut River. Recapping their conversation, Abby said that Mr. Andrews agreed that women with property should be allowed to vote, whereas Abby replied that those women who did not have property needed the vote even more. He left without payment, and apparently the sisters expected to be allowed to get by another year by paying 12 percent interest on the tax. Abby wrote a letter to *The Hartford Courant* about the tax collector's visit, and an article appeared in *The Springfield Republican*, a paper which was very sympathetic to the Smiths and to the cause of suffrage. From here on, the battle with Glastonbury would be fought effectively by the sisters in the press much to the town fathers' chagrin. The host of reporters that would visit the town over the next several years would picture them as a bunch of inept country bumpkins oppressing two vulnerable elderly women in a backwater town.

The next visit by the tax collector would make headlines. On New Year's Day, 1874, Mr. Andrews walked onto the Smiths' property and into the barn that stood just behind the house. There he confiscated seven of the sisters' eight Alderney cows though Julia pleaded with him to leave at least two since one would be distressed if left all alone. Although the sisters asked for a delay until they could once again petition the selectmen to be allowed to vote, the tax collector was not to be put off and began to drive the reluctant seven away. As a reporter for the *Boston Herald* put it "In choosing between the several horns of the dilemma he took seven pairs of horns, with cows attached..." Unfortunately for him, these Alderneys had been raised by Julia and were as much family pets as prized milkers. Each had a name: Jessie, Daisy, Proxy, Minnie, Bessie, Whitey and Lily. When Julia called them, they would come to her at a gallop and when she was outside, they would follow her in single file wherever she led. In fact, according to Abby "when we have had a new tenant they would never, at first, let him come near them, and she has been obliged to stand at their head, where they could see her, every day, when he milked, for ever so long."

Obviously, the situation was much more difficult than Andrews had anticipated. When he tried to lead the cows away, they bellowed and resisted the entire distance to a neighbor's small tobacco shed (fifteen feet by twelve feet as measured by Julia) in which they were to be stabled until the auction. Meanwhile, the one remaining cow, bereft of bovine companionship, set up an unending ruckus that lasted for days, reminding Julia and Abby constantly of their loss. Even after the confiscated cows were safely locked inside the shed, the problems did not end. So contrary did the Alderneys become, the neighbor had to fetch Mr. Kellogg, the Smith's tenant, to come and milk them. To make matters worse for the neighbor, who did not know what he was getting into, his wife would have nothing to do with the milk, saying that not a drop would be allowed into her house since it was as good as stolen. There was also no water near the shed so the besieged neighbor had to carry water a good distance from a well. Abby noted that she and Julia saw him carry twenty-one pails in one day.

While the cows were making life miserable for the unnamed neighbor, the sisters drove to Hartford to consult with their lawyer. They also wrote a letter to the editor of the *Springfield Republican* on January 6, 1874 about the confiscation of their cows and the reasons why they would not pay taxes. It was printed along with an editorial reply in which the editor raised for the first time (but definitely not the last) the parallel between the sister's stand and that taken by the Boston tea party:

> In refusing to continue paying heavier taxes, year by year, than any other property owners in Glastonbury, while refused a voice in assessing and spending them, Abby Smith and her sister as truly stand for the American principle as did the citizens who ripped open the tea-chests in Boston harbor, or the farmers who leveled their muskets at Concord. And they seem to have very much the same quality of quiet, old-fashioned Yankee grit, too. They are not demonstrative or declamatory. They don't shriek, or wring their hands, or make a fuss of any sort. They are good-nature itself. But they are also logic itself, and resolution itself, and pluck itself. They simply stand upon their rights.

The days between January 1 and January 8, 1874, the date set for the auction, dragged by slowly, marked by lowing cows, sleepless nights for Julia (who confessed to a reporter that she felt wretched) and endless treks by the neighbor to the well for water. Finally the day arrived. This time the newspaper headlines were not confined to

Springfield and Hartford but appeared in newspapers in Boston and Providence as well. The story of seven contrary cows, two intransigent elderly spinsters, and one mean-spirited tax collector made wonderful copy.

At noon on that winter day the participants in a strange parade began assembling on Main Street. Their destination was the sign-post about half a mile north, a central gathering place in Glastonbury, where the auction was to be held. First the cows were brought out of the tobacco shed. Tax collector Andrews, at the head of the line, led the best cow. Behind him came the other six cows driven by four men with the help of a dog and a drum. This motley group, bellowing, barking and banging its way along the dirt road, was followed by several carriages and wagons filled with interested spectators and potential bidders. Finally at the end of the possession, Julia and Abby rode in a wagon with Mr. and Mrs. Kellogg, their tenants. When they arrived, about forty men were already waiting at the sign-post hoping to get a good deal on an Alderney. The bids came in very low. For the Smiths, Mr. Kellogg bid for the four best at a price below their value, which covered the tax and the expenses. The remaining three were apparently not sold but were returned to the Smiths. In short, the sisters paid their taxes by buying back their own cows.

The Smiths were shocked by the attitude of the towns people toward them at the auction, stating that "not a man came to speak to us....We would not have believed the town could thus persecute women who were born and bred here..." Yet in fairness to the men at the auction, it is quite possible they bid intentionally low so that Mr. Kellogg could easily bid above them. There was indeed a great reservoir of respect for the Smiths in town and although the reservoir would run low in three or four years, it would never run out. A reporter for the *Boston Globe* interviewing men at one of the town's general stores following the auction said that although none of the men "seemed quite prepared to say that they justified a defiance of the laws as they understood them, all were careful to put themselves in a friendly position to begin with by citing the charity of these sisters, and many stories were told of the suffering that their hands and purses had alleviated."

Julia and Abby did not have much time to ponder their next move since the annual tax was due again in March. This time they were afraid that the tax collector would take personal property such as rugs and artwork. Abby complained in a letter to the *Springfield Republican* that she and her sister might find themselves in the poor house. That this was overstatement is clear from the fact that the Smiths were one of the wealthiest families in Glastonbury owning considerable bank stock and property. When their taxes were increased in 1872, the value of their estate exceeded $10,000.

The statement about their fear of personal property being taken could also be construed as an intentional threat to the town. It was as if the Smiths were goading the tax collector to take their personal property, knowing what a public relations uproar it would cause when prize possessions once belonging to their parents and sisters were carted out the front door. This may explain why Tax Collector Andrews did not seize personal property during the next skirmish as the town had a right to do, but land, which the town did not have a right to do. By law, land could only be seized if there was no personal property of sufficient worth to cover taxes. Were the auctioning of the Alderneys the only battle actually fought between the town and the Smiths, it would be only a humorous anecdote, but from here on the town became more and more heavy-handed in its efforts to collect taxes and the tax collector proved that he and other officials were not above skullduggery in getting what they wanted, thereby confirming by their behavior the Smith's contention that women could be used and misused without adequate means of redress.

*"But the way of the unjust
shall perish. "
Psalm 1:6b*

10

NATIONAL ATTENTION
AND LOCAL ANTAGONISM

At this point the sisters began receiving contributions for a "Defense Fund" from supporters all across the country who had read about the auction of the cows in numerous newspapers. One contributor of five dollars was Isabella Beecher Hooker who wrote with her donation "I am not sure that 'kine couchant' on the grassy slope of the beautiful Connecticut should not be adopted as the emblem of our peaceful suffrage banner -- but however that may be we surely are near the end of our warfare, and God grant that we may use our freedom wisely and well." At the same time, state woman suffrage groups passed resolutions in support of the Smiths' stand. Anonymous poets wrote poems about the auctioning of the cows. One woman collected hairs from the tails of the Alderneys and made them into bouquets of flowers which were sold at a bazaar to raise money for the Smiths. More importantly, nationally known people such as William Lloyd Garrison began to speak out in their defense. The following is an excerpt of a letter from William Lloyd Garrison to Abigail Kelley Foster, the abolitionist leader with whom Hannah had corresponded in the 1840s. Abby Kelley had married and she and her husband were also protesting taxation without representation. The convention to which Garrison refers was to take place in Worcester, Massachusetts, the month following the auction of the Smith cows:

> I see it is announced that among those expected at the meeting are those noble women, the Misses Smith of Glastonbury, Conn. The calm, dignified, uncompromising manner in which they have passed through a similar ordeal entitles them to the warmest sympathy and the highest commendation. The men of Connecticut who can persistently disregard their righteous protest are not worthy to touch the hem of their garments. With all my heart I thank them for what they have done with such admirable judgment, and good sense. Let such examples be multiplied, and it will not be long before the injustice complained of will be remedied, and either there will be no disfranchisement on account of sex, or no taxation where there is no representation.

Julia's speech at the Worcester Convention for Woman's Suffrage underscored the class, race, and religious egalitarianism which permeated her thinking. At that meeting, Julia said that one of the chief arguments the men in Glastonbury raised against allowing women to vote was that it would "let in all the Catholic women and other good for nothing working women. We say, 'do right and let the heavens fall,' leave the consequences with God." Julia and Abby were not fighting to get the vote for themselves only but for all women. They did not fall into the elitist trap of separating out themselves or a certain class of women. The vote should not only be given to propertied single women, it should be extended to all women. In fact, as the Smiths saw it, the vote was even more important for the woman oppressed by a drunkard husband to whom she was but chattel.

The next town meeting which the sisters attended was on April 6, 1874. At about ten o'clock on that early spring morning a carriage pulled up to the town hall where approximately 100 men had gathered to "chew tobacco and compare notes as to the weather and the prospect for the crops." Entering the building, the sisters sat down on a settee to the side of the room while muttering went on among the men to the effect of "Well I wonder what's the trouble now?" and "I don't like to see women unsex themselves." Finally Julia and Abby approached the moderator's desk and asked to be allowed to address the gathering. The moderator refused, informing the sisters that since it was an electors' meeting and the polls must be kept open and unobstructed, he could not legally allow them to speak. Not to be defeated, the Smiths withdrew from the hall, apparently followed by several people who felt that the sisters should have a chance to be heard. Realizing that she could be heard just as well outside as in, Abby mounted an old wagon which stood on the south side of the town hall and taking from her pocket the speech she had prepared, she began to speak. Using the analogy of a family in which both brothers and sisters have property rights which must be respected, Abby asked:

> What do we say of those young men that forsake the society of their sisters, and counsel together without them? We all know their way leads to

ruin. But what should we say if the brothers should by agreement, without consulting their sisters, take their sisters' property from them whenever they chose, and as much as they chose, alleging as an excuse, they had made a law among themselves they would do it. Are their sisters bound by such a law? Are *we* bound by such a law? The case is precisely the same. You all know it is not just.

Although the newspaper correspondent said the crowd was made up of "solid farmers, stalwart laborers, shiftless idlers, young men glad of anything out of the stereotyped order," yet by the end they were respectful and "not a little impressed." When Abby finished, Julia spoke briefly, then they climbed down and mingled with the men, answering questions and countering arguments deftly. One man insisted that there weren't half-a-dozen women in town that wanted to vote, to which Abby replied that those half-dozen should be allowed to vote and the rest could stay away. When one man charged that because they were women they could not fight in wars and could not do road work, Abby archly countered "We could work as well as those did whom we had seen in front of our house, and we would have them fixed very differently too."

In a letter to Lucy Stone, the sisters expressed their bitterness toward the Republicans in town, even having kind words for Tax Collector Andrews, a Democrat, who they considered the actor but not the instigator. Such kind words were not to last, however, for Andrews was not only the tax collector but had been elected one of two representatives to the state legislature, and in that position had the ability to influence lawyers and judges beyond the boundaries of the town, an influence he was not averse to using.

Then on April 11 at three o'clock in the afternoon, the tax collector came again to the Smith household. This time he asked for personal property, but the sisters said they would not aid him in any way. After a discussion in which the sisters restated their case, he said he would attach their land and as required would advertise it nine weeks before it was sold so that the sisters could bid on it if they chose. Accordingly, the following notice was published in the *Hartford Weekly Times*:

> Notice. -- Levied upon by virtue of warrant delivered to me for the collection of taxes for the town of Glastonbury, and so much will be sold at public auction, on Saturday, the 20th day of June, A.D., 1874, at 2 o'clock p.m. on the premises, the following described property, bounded as follows: North on land of Edward A. Horton, east on land of heirs of Hannah H. Smith, south on land of J.N. Hollister, west on the Connecticut River, containing 15 acres, more or less, of meadow land, being the same real estate set in the name of Hannah H. Smith's heirs, on the Glastonbury grand list of 1873, as will pay the following named tax levied thereon and the cost of collection, namely a tax of 5 mills on the dollar, made due and payable on the first day of March, A.D. 1874.
>
> G. C. Andrews, Collector
> Glastonbury, April 13, 1874.

Between that date and the land auction, Lucy Stone asked the sisters to speak at a woman suffrage convention to be held in Lansing, Michigan, but they could not because they were preparing to petition and address the Woman Suffrage Committee of the Connecticut State

Legislature scheduled to meet on May 6th. However, it was not until June 3 that Abby traveled south to New Haven to deliver a hard-hitting speech before the committee. She said that the government had created two classes of citizens, a superior and inferior class and that the sisters as women belonged to the inferior class which was in essence a caste founded on birth as in India, yet more cruel because the classes were not separated, hence women were more aware of the injustice and felt it more keenly. But it was not on the basis of intelligence that this caste existed but on the basis of physical strength. Men were strong enough to put a woman in what they called "her sphere," and then could take her money to be used to maintain their rights and her confinement. She then argued that women were better citizens than men; after all, 228 men and only two women filled the state prisons. Furthermore, it was men who filled the grog shops and then inflicted physical abuse on women in the homes, by which Abby implied that women needed the vote so that they could outlaw alcohol, thereby improving the quality of their lives markedly. She ended her speech by pointing out that the Fourteenth Amendment to the Constitution used the words "persons" and "citizens," not "men" or "male." Since no state could deprive *any person* of life, liberty or property without due process of law, nor deny to any person within its jurisdiction the equal protection of the laws, then Connecticut was acting criminally.

Her speech was not well received. There was no applause at its end, though the two women who spoke next did receive applause, whereas Abby remarked acidly that they were married women and probably knew how to please men better than did she and Julia. The Legislature gave the sisters no answer and one month later gave them "leave to withdraw" their petition which asked for the right to vote. This the sisters found insulting. It harkened back to the gag rule on abolition against which they had fought so fiercely in the 1830s and 1840s. As Julia cynically put it, she and her sister discovered they *did* have rights after all: the right to deliver speeches from carts, and the right to withdraw petitions.

With the sale of their land looming, the sisters consulted two lawyers in Hartford who told them that it was illegal for the town to seize land, that moveable estate (personal property) must be levied first, and only if that were insufficient could land be taken. As had been posted, the sisters went to the fifteen acres at the appointed time of two o'clock. When the tax collector finally showed up an hour late, they told him the sale of the land was illegal. He caught them off-guard by saying that the land had already been bargained for, but if the sisters still wished to bid they could. They refused on the grounds that to do so would be to consent to an unlawful deed, whereas the tax collector called out twice for another bid. Receiving none, he struck off the auction. When the sisters asked who had bid, he said Nelson Hardin who owned the farm north of the Smiths, a man the sisters said had "been trying to get our land by moving bounds between us, and other outrageous acts, so that there was no living beside him without going to law." The sisters took comfort in the fact that no other man in town had bid on the land apparently because they did not countenance such a low-lived act:

Mr. H. and three others to measure off the eleven acres, were all that were there, except two of our neighbors who accompanied us, and not one of us heard the land bid off at all. It must have been before our premises were reached, and the advertisement said it was to be sold on the premises. We have now but four acres of meadow land left, and the poorest part too. Meadow land

sells for $150 to $200 per acre, so that nearly
$2,000 worth was disposed of for $78.35. ...This
is a deed that we could not have believed even the
man that so ruthlessly seized our cows could have
been persuaded to do.

Shortly after the seizure of their land, the sisters went
to see their lawyer in Hartford, but he kept putting them
off, telling them he was too busy and to return in two or
three weeks. When the sisters tenaciously did so, he was
even cooler, saying he had talked to the tax collector, who,
as has been pointed out, was at this time a member of the
State Legislature, and that the tax collector had said the
sisters had denied having any personal property and that,
furthermore, the sisters were Hannah Smith's heirs.
According to a contrived legal argument, since she had
died many years before, the only estate remaining had to
be real estate, hence the seizure of the meadow lands was
legal. But the house was filled with furniture and art
stretching back to the family's first days in town, and the
barn was loaded with hay, as well as the wood shed with
wood, to say nothing of the cows. The seizure was also
unconscionable because no matter what value the sisters put
on the meadow land, there was no doubt that it was the
best agricultural soil on the entire three-mile stretch.
Andrews could easily have gotten the tax by selling off less
valuable land.

Six times the sisters drove into Hartford. Finally their
lawyer told them to pay the taxes, or if they persisted in
wanting to bring suit, to get another lawyer. He stated that
the town, in case it was decided against them, would carry
it up through every court, even to the court of errors. The
sisters wondered how he could have known what the town
was going to do unless he had spoken to town officials,
which indeed he had in talking to the tax collector.

Realizing that their lawyer had no intention of fighting their case, the sisters immediately employed another lawyer who brought suit against the tax collector for trespass and illegal sale. The trial of suit was held at the house of Judge Hollister about a mile south of the Smiths on Main Street. One reporter described the scene as follows:

> Approaching Justice Hollister's, a little off the main street, there were signs of people stirring about. In front of the house stood a row of teams, betokening some unwonted occurrence within. The inside itself presented a bit of picturesque groupings worthy the brush of a Hogarth. Through an ample hall-way opened the sitting room, connected with yet another room by folding doors. In the latter, around a table, sat those immediately interested in the case. The justice of the peace, an exceedingly quiet, home-spun gentleman, with short, grey hair, occupied the most conspicuous place, and chewed a lead pencil and nervously rubbed his chin as the lawyers with flattering unction sandwiched in their "your honors." Flanking him on either side were the attorneys for the plaintiff and defendant, shrewd and tenacious and both deeply versed in the noble art of bothering and befogging witnesses. Grouped about were the principal witnesses, the unlucky tax-collector, tall and angular -- a good specimen of the modern Yankee -- the surveyor and his assistants, who measured off the disputed land, various town officials, with countenances expressive of grave interest, and last, but not least, the two heroines of the play. They are dressed in prim but genteel black, and sit beside each other, keenly watching the slow unfolding of

the plot. Abby is the taller of the two, thin and straight as a lath, and sits erect in her cane-bottomed chair through the tedious hours with less signs of weariness than a modern girl in her teens would show. Julia, the elder, is more petite, and shows less indications of age, if anything, than her sister. Notwithstanding she is nearly 80 years, her face is still bright and expressive, and she evidently entered into the occasional humor of the affair more heartily than Abby. At first, both were restive under the hatcheling of the cross-examination and the petty sparring of the lawyers, and uttered an impatient protest, but as the hours wore on, they settled down into heroic resignation.

The reporter's description of the gathered crowd was also fascinating. Apparently they were all male except for Mrs. Kellogg, the one female witness, and "a couple of young ladies, who furtively listened to proceedings through the open door of an adjoining parlor." On the uncomfortable wooden benches sat about 20 men in the outer room, chiefly farmers "in their shirt-sleeves, fresh from the rowen field and the potato patch":

The miller, well powered [sic] with flour, edged his way in for an entertaining and profitable nooning. Several small boys and embarrassed youths, with clean paper-collars atop of soiled shirts, looked on with awe-struck countenances, and consoled themselves with peanuts on the sly during the earlier intervals. Indeed, the awesome way with which the spectators, both young and old, evinced their sense of the majesty of the law was quite oppressive. It was contagious, and a thoughtless little black-and-tan terrier, that strayed into the court, slunk guiltily under a bench beneath the influence.

Horace Cornwall of Hartford represented the sisters and W.S. Goslee of Glastonbury represented the town. Since the law was clear that moveable property had to be seized before real estate, the tax collector insisted that there was no moveable property which the sisters maintained was an out-and-out lie. "He saw no furniture, though sitting in our best furnished rooms, and had to confess, in answer to our able lawyer, that he looked not for wood in the woodhouse, nor for hay in the barn, nor did he even step over the way to inquire of the tenant whether there was stock on the farm, and he was expressly told that we owned the cows in the yard." The case went from ten a.m. until six p.m. during which time Mr. Goslee repeatedly "poured forth a bitter tirade" against the sisters. According to Julia "he threatened us terribly about the consequences when this tax would be laid again. It would be much worse for us than if we had paid for all this case." Disregarding Goslee's ranting, Judge Hollister ruled in favor of the sisters and awarded them ten dollars in damages as well as cost for a total of $28.52. But the sisters were not allowed to savor their hard-won victory because Mr. Goslee immediately appealed the case to the next court in Hartford.

During the intervals between the trials, the sisters were extremely busy: traveling to Rhode Island in October to deliver a speech to the Rhode Island Suffrage Society at its annual meeting; attending town meetings; answering letters by the hundreds. Finally in February 1875, the time came for the town's appeal. The weather was cold and bad which did not prevent Julia and Abby from traveling back and forth from Glastonbury to Hartford for the three days of the trial. Again the tax collector contended he took land because there was not sufficient personal property, whereas the Smiths along with Mrs. Kellogg made clear the extent of their personal holdings. One of the town's lawyers complained that the Smiths were giving the town a bad name and that they were taking up valuable court space and time. In response, the Smiths' lawyer pointed out that the sisters were not the ones who had appealed the case; therefore, it was the town that was taking up valuable space and wasting the state's time. Having heard the presentation of fact, the judge deferred his decision. Julia charged that the deferral was intentional so that his decision could not be appealed to the Court of Errors for the March session. Furthermore, she accused the town of tinkering with the judicial system by setting "up a judge of their own, removing the regular one, and substituting in his stead, another whom they had reason to think would decide as they wish to have him." Speaking at the Melrose Convention several weeks after the case was heard, she said that the judge "promised Mr. Cornwall, our lawyer, to give him the facts in the case. Our lawyer followed him from day to day, and can get nothing from him, for he says the papers are all lost and he remembers nothing about it. Our lawyer wrote down some of the facts, but he would not assent to them, for it seems to be the intention of the other side, to foil us entirely from bringing the case to the court of errors even so late as next fall." Finally the judge ruled against the Smiths, agreeing with the town that there was no personal property to be seized, hence the taking of the land was legal. Although it was in fact too late for the case to be heard by fall, Mr. Cornwall, the Smiths' lawyer immediately brought suit against the town, the collector, and Hardin who had a deed to the meadow land, to bring the case before the Court of Equity to set aside the deed.

In the year and a half period before the third trial took

place in the Court of Equity, the town attempted to get an ex post facto law called the "General Healing Act" passed by the state legislature to sanction the taking of land for back taxes. Julia, ever able to match wits, said that if anybody needed a healing act, it was she and her sister, for their rights and their feelings had been sufficiently disturbed to require healing. This was a game of point/counterpoint. The town reseized the cows and advertised the auction to be held on April 15, 1876, whereas the sisters invited everyone to come and "take some refreshments at their home, as they still hold the old mansion." Two days later the town sold in Hartford at the public signpost near the old State House one share of stock in Phoenix National Bank which they had seized from the sisters. The published announcement of the sale did not mention to whom the stock belonged, an oversight which the sisters swiftly corrected by writing to both the *Hartford Daily Times* and the *Hartford Daily Courant*. Whatever the town officials tried to do surreptitiously, the sisters made overt. "Yesterday we went to Hartford through the floods and attended the auction, against the advise of our lawyer, who said women did not go to auctions, but we do not let our property be sacrificed in this way without seeing to it, neither do we let it pass without talking of robbery." During this same period, someone maliciously sent a notice to the *Hartford Daily Post* saying that the Smiths' lawyer had appeared in Glastonbury and settled the tax for them. Mr. Cornwall was forced to write a denial to the paper.

To add insult to injury, the town again seized cows in November of that year taking a little calf and its mother much to the sisters' dismay. Julia wrote the following account to the *Woman's Journal*:

> The 23d inst., at 2 o'clock P.M. the sale at the signpost was to take place, and we were on hand

in due time. Though it rained, the collector waited for the first select man and two justices of the peace to make their appearance. He then set up the cow and calf, and had a man of his own to bid several times very low, and added a dollar more at a time. To put an end to this business I bid $120, and told the collector I supposed it was enough to cover the tax and cost, the tax being ninety-six dollars and sixty-five cents. He set up another cow at once, which was struck off to me for forty-one dollars, the amount for the two being $161. I had but $125 with me, and said, as he was coming up to our house, that I could pay it at home, but he immediately called out that the cows were not sold, and set them right up again, and he would take no bid of ours the second time, and we got Mr. Kellogg to bid, but he had no cash with him. At last he ordered me to go home and get it, giving twenty-five minutes time to go three-quarters of a mile. By the fleetness of Mr. Kellogg's horse we did get back within one minute of the time, though I went to a neighbor's to get a little more, for I knew perfectly well if I failed by only fifty cents, all our stock would at once be sacrificed, for he held watch in hand, and a neighbor heard him say the time was about out.

This was also the year that Julia was preparing her Bible translation for publication. Although her principal reason was to prove beyond a shadow of a doubt that women were the intellectual equals of men, she also admitted that the fame it would bring her might make her something besides Abby Smith's sister.

While antagonisms continued to brew on the local level, among suffrage circles the Smith sisters were acclaimed nationally. A generation older than the leaders of the movement including Elizabeth Cady Stanton and Lucy Stone, the Smiths were treated like elder states-women who tied the movement historically with the American Revolution. Julia and Abby obligingly filled this role to the point of naming one of their Alderney calves Abigail Adams and another Martha Washington. They were eagerly sought as convention speakers and although they had never traveled much in their entire lives, they boarded trains and carriages in the middle of winter and the bleakest of weather bound for distant cities. In January 1876, the beginning of the nation's centennial year, Julia was the center of attention at the eighth annual convention of the National Woman Suffrage Association held in Washington, D.C.. When asked to speak at a reception given in her honor by Jane Spofford at the Riggs House, she humorously related:

> There are but two of our cows left at present, Taxey and Votey. It is something a little peculiar that Taxey is very obtrusive; why, I can scarcely step out of doors without being confronted by her, while Votey is quiet and shy, but she is growing more docile and domesticated every day, and it is my opinion that in a very short time, wherever you find Taxey there Votey will be also.

No wonder the Smiths were so popular among suffragists. As serious as they were about the cause, they never lost their sense of humor. It was impossible for newspaper editors to resist the thought of two cows named Taxey and Votey, or a calf named Abigail Adams.

Finally the time came for the third trial at the Court of Equity on November 1876 before Judge McManus. This time the ruling was in their favor and the town chose not to appeal again. It was hardly a glorious victory for Julia and Abby because all they had proven was that the tax collector had the right to seize their personal property but not their land. They did not get a reprieve from paying taxes, nor did they receive the vote. Yet they had made it clear to the town that they would continue to make life difficult for every male selectman and registrar who denied them their rights.

In January 1878, the National Woman Suffrage Association decided again to work for passage of a constitutional amendment for woman suffrage. Traveling to Washington D.C. for the NWSA convention, Julia, then 85 years old, spoke before the Congressional Committee on Privileges and Elections, telling of the trials that she and Abby had literally and figuratively gone through in Glastonbury. "This is the first time in my life that I have trod these halls, and what has brought me here? I say oppression -- oppression of women by men." She asked that the Committee report to the Senate in favor of the Sixteenth Amendment so that women in the United States would be saved the desecration of their homes which the Smiths had suffered.

When Julia returned to Glastonbury, she and Abby drafted yet another petition for the Connecticut General Assembly. Their energy seemed boundless: speeches, confrontations with town officials, letters to supporters, petitions, interviews with reporters. Then in July it all came to an end. On July 23, 1878 Abby died at the age of 81, leaving only Julia. As the obituary in *The Hartford Post* said, "her sister has lost her chief support, and the community in which she lived a faithful friend and a worthy exponent of the virtues of truthfulness, firmness, and adherence to the right as she understood it." Abby had written the following lyrics for a hymn in her latter years:

Fear not: our great Redeemer lives
    And lo from death shall set us free.
Tho' now we die, if we are his
    These very eyes the Lord shall see.

Now 86 years old, Julia had not been alone a day in her entire life. She had always been the cerebral member of the family, the one who most liked the quietude of her study, the comfort of her books. Although she had been as vocal as Abby and never walked in her shadow, yet it was Abby who was the more social. Abby may have been set free from death by the Redeemer, as she wished, but Julia was locked in grief.

*"And sat not in the seat
of those scoffing."
Psalm 1:1*

11

A BITTER EPILOGUE

After Abby's death, Julia did not know what to do. The old drafty house was far too large for one elderly woman to live in. Every room, every corner, reminded her that she was alone. Family mementoes stretched back to the French and Indian War; furniture from the Federalist period sat below Laurilla's sketches and paintings. Even worse, there were the huge Erastus Salisbury Field portraits staring down at her: Hannah in her frilled cap, Zephaniah with his hand on the law book, her sisters in their black dresses with the mutton-leg sleeves. Of all her sisters, she had been closest to Abby. When Abby was born, five-year-old Julia had resented her because her arrival meant Julia had lost her exalted position as the family baby. But from the time that Julia accepted her position as fourth in the line of daughters but first in her father's heart because of her intellectual nature, the two sisters had been almost inseparable, forming a dyad in the midst of the family circle. Shortly after Abby's death, Julia sent a postcard to Susan B. Anthony in which she spoke of their special relationship:

> My dear sympathizing friend. How can I indeed bear the loss of so dear a friend. We two were one all our long lives. You will accept of this card I know in answer to your touching letter for how can I write at all. It is a comfort to have loving friends remember us in our affliction and I had Mrs. Hooker and Miss Burr to help sustain my heart stricken spirit but it takes a higher power to heal the wound. You have had sisters and can have some idea how they cling to each other but you know not what it is to be the last one of such an affectionate family. Abby had more courage than I and was more decided and would have known what to do had she been left alone. But as yet I have made no plan how I shall get along. Some cousins from Vermont came on purpose to take me home with them the day after the funeral but I could not go for a while. I have my mind. I must do necessary business. I may possibly go next week. With sincere thanks for your kind remembrance. Yours with a heart overflowing with grief.

As she had said she would, Julia kept busy, answering personally the letters of sympathy which poured in from all across the country. One letter came from a man named Amos Parker (often referred to as Judge Amos Parker), an elderly lawyer from Fitzwilliam, New Hampshire. Julia not only responded but sent him a copy of her book *Abby Smith and Her Cows*, on the inside cover of which was an advertisement for her Bible. Amos Parker wrote back inquiring about it and a friendship began to develop via letter. Writing that it would be easier to discuss the Bible with her in person, he came for a visit; the outcome was a marriage proposal. Apparently Julia herself was as surprised as the rest of the town. In a letter to Isabella Beecher Hooker on April 27, 1879, she said "But none can be more surprised than I myself am, that I should enter into a married state at this time of life and it has taken me a good while to decide, though I have corresponded with the gentleman almost ever since Abby's death, but when I saw you last I did not think such an event would take place." In the obituary that Francis Ellen Burr wrote for *The Hartford Times* after Julia's death, she recounted that Julia asked her advice about getting married at her age because she was afraid she would become the laughing stock of the world. Burr said that it didn't matter:

> That is the least important thing about it. How long will the comments last? Perhaps a week, for the world cannot afford to give more than that to anyone, no matter how noted. You are alone. This matter concerns you and not the world. The world's praise or blame ought not to have a feather's weight in the matter. "Well," [Julia] replied, "I was in hopes you would ridicule me roundly, and advise me not to marry, for your doing so would have prevented me.

Although Amos Parker was himself 86 years old, he wore a brown wig which gave at least one Smith relative the impression that he was trying to look younger. According to friends of the Smiths, he was a bit of a braggart who enjoyed telling about accompanying General Lafayette from Boston to Concord during the General's American tour in 1825, being the son of a United States Senator, and having close relatives who had died on Revolutionary War battlefields. A widower twice over, Amos Parker was in good health, attributing it to total abstinence from "any stimulants, narcotics or tobacco tea or coffee." He would, in fact, live to be 101 years and 7 months and was until the very end spry and talkative.

Their marriage, less than nine months after Abby's death, was quiet and private. Given Julia's firm stand against ministers, it is surprising that the ceremony was performed by Rev. William Scudder of First Church. But the neighbors and friends, who were deeply fond of her, could not let such a momentous occasion go by without celebration, and so on Friday evening April 25, 1879, they threw an enormous reception for the newlyweds, complete with wedding cake, music and dancing. It was almost a complete surprise to Mr. and Mrs. Parker. Julia wrote to Isabella Beecher Hooker shortly thereafter that she only found out about it because the hosts needed to know what time Amos Parker would be returning from Hartford. Mrs. Hooker, though unable to attend, had received the following invitation:

Dear Madame, The pleasure of your company is requested at a party to be given by the ladies of this neighborhood; at the residence of Mrs. Julia E. Smith Parker, in honor of her marriage. To be given Friday evening, April 25th, 1879. Very Respectfully Edward W. Hale.

Because of the fame of the Smith family, reporters showed up at the reception, unable to forego writing stories about a feisty suffragette becoming the octogenarian virgin bride of a bewigged judge who had traveled with Lafayette. It was almost as good a story as bellowing pet bovines being sold for back taxes.

According to the *Hartford Courant* reporter, on that spring evening:

The procession was headed by the bride and groom, who were escorted to the seat of honor, at which had been placed the two old Saltonstall plates and cups, formerly owned by Governor Saltonstall of Connecticut, for 200 years a possession of the Smith family..."Almost as old as we are," remarked Julia, in her quaint, humorous way.

The reporter remarked that the Smith piano used for the occasion sounded like a violin because of its age, but "As everything was on an antique order from the bride and groom down, nothing could have been more appropriate in the way of accompaniment. A number of people encouraged the bride and groom to dance, but while Amos was willing and Julia was able, she said that if she did, it would get into the papers and "she didn't wish folks to say she had gone to pieces completely." Besides the music, there were all kinds of foods and fruits with tea and coffee and to top it all off, there was "a most elegant pyramid" with the couple's names in gilt letters.

But the bride and groom were not to live happily ever after. In fact, the reception seems to have been the last happy, humorous event in Julia's life. Prior to Amos Parker's appearance, Julia had apparently encouraged the cousin, who had invited her to come to Vermont following Abby's death, to move to Glastonbury in order to help her take care of the farm in her declining years. With the clear understanding that he would inherit the farm after her death, Horace Smith moved his family to the house directly across the road which Laurilla had built for tenants some years previously. But after her marriage, Julia apparently reneged on the agreement and ordered Horace Smith to leave the house and farm into which he had already invested time and money. He brought suit against the Parkers claiming he had an oral contract. The judge ruled in Julia's favor much to the dismay of many townspeople who had come to like Horace Smith. Close friends of Julia's were aghast at this turn of affairs. Feeling that she had wronged Horace Smith, thirty of them petitioned Julia in writing stating:

> We the citizens of Glastonbury, who have heretofore honored the name and character of Julia E. Smith, Now, by reason of these transactions of hers, feel that she has brought discredit upon her former good character, and thereby forfeited that respect which she has held for so many years.

Included among the signers were many devoted friends of the Smiths in happier times. But the strongly worded petition succeeded only in raising Julia's ire. Even her dearest friend Emily Moseley, who had met with her weekly during the years Julia was translating the Bible, and whom Julia considered "the second mourner" at Abby's funeral, wrote to her in protest:

> My once dear friend, Yes it was so for as Julia E. Smith, you were a dear & highly valued friend but now that you are Mrs.Parker I cannot find it in my heart to say it in truth -- Why is it? Does intimate connection with a man necessarily produce such a change of character as seems to be evident in your case? If so, I may be more thankful than ever that I have happily escaped the influence. Perhaps however it is not that your character has suffered but that some hidden motive has induced a change of action only -- It is to be hoped that the cause of your recent unreasonable conduct has no deeper foundation than impulse, stimulated by some outside influence.

The outside influence Emily was referring to was Amos Parker himself whom she and other Smith friends found to be self-centered and pompous. Although they had all wished the pair well at the beginning of their marriage as was made clear by their hosting such a wonderful reception, many of the friends became suspicious shortly thereafter that Amos Parker had married Julia Smith merely to inherit her considerable wealth so that he could pass it on to his children.

Julia's response to Emily's letter was venomous, "people do sometimes change in mind and character without changing the name. It must be so in your case." She claimed that she wrote out several wills and that Horace Smith's name did not appear until after Abby's death. Claiming she was not "always under [Mr. Parker's] influence," she said "Mr. Parker and I believe each other perfectly truthful, I know he is by daily observation as he never varies from the truth in the least item and we have as good a right to assert our belief as you have yours." At the end of the letter she said "I do not desire the friendship of anyone who will desert me in the time of trouble and try to blackmail me by threatening to destroy my character." That such a long-standing deep friendship could come to such a bitter end is indicative of the mistrust and rancor which sprang up at the end of Julia's life.

In spite of the pleas of friends, Horace Smith was forced to leave the farm, moving to another home in Glastonbury. Then on April 23, 1884, the unthinkable occurred -- the contents of the house were auctioned off under Judge Amos Parker's orders. Listed among the many items on the broadside advertising the auction were a London-made piano, a large looking-glass, an antique case of drawers, furniture, 8-10 cords of seasoned firewood, a two-seater carriage, and 50 Bibles. Some of Julia's possessions, including the Erastus Salisbury Field paintings, eventually found their way to the Mitchels in South Britain, Connecticut, but many items were sold to strangers. The Parkers moved first to a house in the nearby town of Newington and then to the Parkville section of Hartford.

As for the tax battle, that too came to an inglorious conclusion. After the marriage, the taxes on the Glastonbury house and farm were dutifully paid by Amos Parker, since Julia said she would not pay them with her own money. However, according to one memoir, many months after he had paid the bill, she handed him a package which she said was a present. Inside was the exact amount of the taxes.

However, marriage and her very advanced years did not extinguish completely her fighting spirit. In a letter to Isabella Hooker written just a few weeks after her marriage, Julia said that she thought Amos would be a "great help in our great reform." Although that was not to be the case, he did not hinder her in taking part in suffrage activities. In fact, at the age of 91, she attended the state convention of the Connecticut State Suffrage Association in March 1884, at which she "gave an extemporaneous talk to the great delight of the audience, who applauded continually" according to Frances Ellen Burr.

Although it is not certain that Julia herself came to mistrust Amos Parker, there is one piece of evidence which suggests that she may have had misgivings. In a copy of her Bible, she left the following note. "Julia E. Smith to be buried between L.A. Smith and A.H. Smith; her name as before marriage and birth and death inscribed on the gravestone in the same manner as her sisters."

On November 7, 1885, Julia fell and badly shattered her hip while living in Hartford. The doctor concluded that because of her age and the severity of the break, the hip could not be reset. She died four months later on March 6,

1886. Not long before her death, she told Francis Ellen
Burr that she did not like to draw her curtains in her home
for she loved the light streaming in. "I never liked the
night. Oh if I can only find a place where there is no more
night!"

As if all the bitterness of the last few years of her life
was too great to be confined by the grave, after her death
there was disagreement about her will because her entire
estate of about $8,000 was left to Amos Parker, then 92
years old. A newspaper article said that "A codicil to the
will revokes several bequests originally made. The codicil
is in Mr. Parker's handwriting but the signature is clearly
the testator's." Another article published several weeks
later said that the Probate Court had asked Amos Parker to
produce an earlier will seen by Mrs. Kellogg, Julia's close
friend from Glastonbury. According to the article:

> It is known that his wife made a will subsequently
> to this one, in which she practically cut him off
> for the reasons that he had deceived her, as she
> said, in many ways. When they moved from
> Glastonbury to Newington he wanted her to have
> the deed of the property in the latter place made in
> his name. She told him that her money was to pay
> for it, and he studied over the matter, but he said
> he would reconvey the place to her, and she did as
> he wished, but subsequently he refused to keep his
> promise. This and other experiences convinced her
> that all he cared for was to get possession of her
> property and that that was what he married her
> for. The latest will was on her table one day, and
> a little while after she missed it and inquiring of
> Parker if he had seen it he said that he had put it
> away. After that she was taken ill, and it proved
> to be the last sickness. The conversation she had

at the time referred to was in the presence of a lady friend.

When Amos produced the old will after her death, the probate court asked if he knew of another will. He said he did not, but apparently changed his story when the eye witness, Mrs. Kellogg, came forward. He then said that he did know of another will but that Julia had destroyed it.

So the final chapter of the Smith family's eventful lives came to an end. Amos Parker moved back to Fitzwilliam, New Hampshire where he would live until 101. Julia was buried as she had requested in Glastonbury among her beloved family, which was the only place she had ever wanted to be. Only her maiden name is on the headstone.

Writing about a visit she had made to the Smiths, Lucy Stone said:

As I went through the rooms where these brave women live, it seemed to me that the spot whereon I trod was holy ground. Here began a peaceful resistance to the same kind of tyranny as that which caused the Revolution, and here, some day, as to Bunker Hill now, will come men and women who are reverent of the great principle of the consent of the governed, who respect courage and fidelity to principle, and who will hold at its true value, the part which these sisters have taken in solving the meaning of a representative government.

No such veneration was to take place however, and the entire Smith family passed into history, earning themselves only occasional footnotes. To this day, their tax battle is too often seen as an amusing anecdote -- an unimportant fight carried on by cantankerous spinsters -- instead of a brave stand by two elderly women who had everything to lose, and, at their age, little to gain. Another thirty-four years would go by before the 19th Amendment would pass in 1920 allowing women to vote. Neither did their abolition activities bring them any personal satisfaction or fame. As for Julia's Bible, copies ended up gathering dust in Glastonbury attics. Called derisively "the Alderney Edition" after the cows sold at auction, the translation never received any serious scholarly attention. Yet even had they been able to foresee the failure of their various causes, it would not have changed their course of action. The Smiths took as the heavenly template for their earthly lives the following scripture from the third chapter of Galations, as translated by Julia: "There is neither Jew nor Greek, there is neither servant nor free, there is neither male and female; for ye are all one in Christ Jesus."

REFERENCE NOTES

INTRODUCTION

Page 1, QUOTE

David Donald, *Lincoln Reconsidered* (New York: Vintage Books, 1961), 22.

CHAPTER 1 -- HANNAH HADASSAH SMITH

Page 7, SOUTH BRITAIN

South Britain is now part of Southbury, CT. Early in its history Southbury was called Woodbury.

Page 7, HICKOK

The name Hickok is spelled several different ways. Hannah herself spelled it "Hickok," but David spelled it "Hicock." However, it is spelled "Hicok" on his tombstone, and is listed as "Hickox" in some of the early records.

Page 7, YALE

Many accounts list David as a Yale graduate but in a letter dated April 3, 1854 to Mr. Cothren, the author of *The History of Ancient Woodbury*, Julia wrote that David had obtained a "perfect knowledge of [French] while a member of Yale College, though he did not study to take a degree on account of ill health, he was a very learned man & a great mathematician." Smith Papers, Historical Society of Glastonbury.

Page 8, FREEDOM

Nancy F. Cott, *The Bonds of Womanhood, "Woman's Sphere" in New England, 1780-1835*, (New Haven and London: Yale

University Press, 1977), 5-6. Nancy Cott states that the ideology of domesticity forced women to play a limited and sex-specific role by the 1830s: "When white manhood suffrage, stripped of property qualifications, became the rule, women's political incapacity appeared more conspicuous than it had in the colonial period. As occupations in trade, crafts, and services diversified the agricultural base of New England's economy, and wage earning encroached on family farm production, women's second-class position in the economy was thrown into relief. There was only a limited number of paid occupations generally open to women, in housework, handicrafts and industry, and school-teaching. Their wages were one-fourth to one-half what men earned in comparable work. The legal handicaps imposed by the marriage contract prevented wives from engaging in business ventures of their own, and the professionalization of law and medicine by means of educational requirements, licensing, and professional societies severely excluded women from those avenues of distinction and earning power. Because colleges did not admit women, they could not enter any of the learned professions. For them, the Jacksonian rhetoric of opportunity had scant meaning."

Page 10, **SPIN WOOL**

There are no primary records about Abigail Mitchel during Hannah's childhood other than occasional references in David Hickok's diary. However, although Hannah's intellectual prowess was always attributed to her father, her relationship with her mother seems to have been a warm one. Though the Smiths moved to Glastonbury over 50 miles to the northeast, there was much visiting back and forth and letter-writing. In fact, Abigail spent the last twelve years of her life living with the Smiths after the death of her second husband Eleazer Mitchel. When she died on February 11, 1831, Julia wrote "it was a good day when I got up but I did not find our grandmother better. At nine o'clock she appeared to have her reason perfectly. She seemed so ill that Abby told her that she was afraid that she would not be able to live. She wanted to live she said, but she was not able to pray. Our grandmother died at eleven o'clock. I shall never be able to forget those last moments. Is it possible that she is gone? It is nearly twelve years since she came to live with us. Although she was nearly ninety-two years old we weep as if she were much younger. Her death has been sudden and unexpected. Pray to God that he pity us and we be given grace to bear all the afflictions which he sends us and may we be prepared to leave this world..." Mary Helen Kidder, "The Sisters Smith of Glastonbury: Intellectuals, Rebels & Cranks," 1937, Mss. Connecticut Historical Society, Hartford, Ct., 8.

Page 10, **CONTRIBUTIONS**

William Kingsley, ed., *Contributions to The Ecclesiastical History of Connecticut* (New Haven: William L. Kingsley, J.H. Benham, Printer, 1861), 477.

Page 12, **BRITISH RAIDS**

British raids actually did occur on several towns including Danbury, Ridgefield and West Haven, all of which were not far from South Britain. Fairfield County and the lower part of Litchfield County, in which South Britain was located, were heavily Tory in part because there were many Episcopalians in the area. President Ezra Stiles of Yale estimated that one fourth of the citizens of Fairfield County were loyalists. In fact, the town of Ridgefield actually voted on January 3, 1775 to repudiate the Continental Congress, sentiments which Newtown shared. Albert E. Van Dusen, *Connecticut*, (New York: Random House, 1961), 141.

Another reason why there were many loyalists in this area was because of the influence of a Scottish theologian named Robert Sandeman who preached that the Bible required believers to remain loyal to whatever government was in place, not dissenting in any way. As will be seen, his thinking deeply affected the Smiths, for it would be to Newtown that Zephaniah would come as a new minister.

Page 14, **CLOCKS**

On August 20 and 29, 1844, Hannah wrote in her diary that

she had taken apart and was rebuilding the clock belonging to her daughter Cyrinthia.

Page 15, **DIARY ENTRY**

Reference to 65 years may be incorrect in this entry for it would have meant Hannah's father was dead in 1782 when she was fifteen. She noted elsewhere that she was seventeen when her father died.

Page 16, **TEACHING**

The practice of women teaching summer school was not uncommon in the eighteenth century. Such schools were often for very young children and girls.

CHAPTER 2 -- ZEPHANIAH HOLLISTER SMITH

Page 18, **BIRTH DATE**

The Glastonbury Vital Records list Zephaniah's birth as August 21, 1759 whereas the gravestone has August 19, 1758.

Page 18, **HOLLISTER FAMILY**

Lieutenant John Hollister, ca 1612-1665, was a direct ancestor of Zephaniah's through his mother, Ruth Hollister. John Hollister was a settler in Wethersfield, of which Glastonbury was then a part. In 1656 he instigated a petition to the General Court calling for the dismissal of Rev. John Russell from the Wethersfield Society. The disagreement involved conflicting forms of church polity. The outcome was that Rev. Russell left the church in 1659. Marjorie McNulty, *Glastonbury From Settlement to Suburb*, (Glastonbury, CT: The Historical Society of Glastonbury, 1983), 11-12.

The names of Zephaniah's brothers and sisters were Asa Smith, Achsah (Axa), Elizur, Ruth, Hannah and Jemima. Jemima died when she was three years old. Glastonbury Vital Records.

Page 18, **YALE IN GLASTONBURY**

According to McNulty, students were also sent to Farmington and Wethersfield. Among the students in Glastonbury were Noah Webster, Joel Barlow, Oliver Wolcott, Jr., Uriah Tracy, and Zephaniah Swift. Marjorie McNulty, "Yale Classes Held Here in Revolutionary Wartime," *The Publick Post*, (Glastonbury, CT: The Historical Society of Glastonbury, 1987), 2-3.

Page 19, **YALE DURING WAR**

The information on Yale during the Revolution comes from Louis L. Tucker, *Connecticut's Seminary of Sedition: Yale College*, (Cheshire: Pequot Press, 1974), 53-66, and from *The Literary Diary of Ezra Stiles*, edited by Franklin Bowditch Dexter, (New York: Charles Scribner & Sons, 1901).

Page 20, **GEORGE WELLES**

A picture of George Welles leading the battle was drawn by St. John Honeywell and is included in *The Literary Diary of Ezra Stiles*, Vol. II. See also Tucker, 68.

Page 20, **WAR SERVICE OF ISAAC AND ASA SMITH**

As to the war service of Isaac and Asa Smith, Isaac served under Col. David Waterbury in the 1st Company of the Fifth Connecticut Regiment from May 8, 1775 to December 13, 1775. *Record of Service of Connecticut Men in the War of the Revolution*, Connecticut Adjutants General, Hartford, 1889.

Asa joined in April 1777, regular service, under Ensign George Smith of Glastonbury. He served in the company commanded by Capt. Elijah Wright in the regiment commanded by Col. Samuel Walker. In August 1777 he was taken sick and sent home. In September 1777, his father, Isaac, hired a substitute named Samuel Manly to take his place in the regular service. "Asa Smith -- Revolutionary War Pension Application," Floyd Country, Indiana, Court of the Board of Commissioners, January, 1834. Pension granted #S

32528. (This information was collected by William M. Bailey, a descendent of Asa Smith's.)

Page 20, **ELIZUR GOODRICH**

Tucker, *Connecticut's Seminary of Sedition*, 61.

Page 21, **STILES QUOTE**

Ibid., 66.

Page 22, **DEBATE TOPICS**

The Literary Dairy of Ezra Stiles, 1,6,8,19,20,31.

Page 23, **LICENSED TO PREACH**

William Kingsley, *Contributions to the Ecclesiastical History of Connecticut*, (New Haven: William L. Kingsley, J.H. Benham, Printer, 1861), 311, 343.

Page 25, **SOME THOUGHTS**

"Some Thoughts on Christianity in a Letter to a Friend by Mr. Sandeman, author of the Letters on Theron and Aspasio To which is Annexed By Way of Illustration The Conversion of Jonathan the Jew As Related by Himself" was published in Boston by W.M. Alpine and J. Fleeming in Marlborough MDXIV. It is contained in Early American Imprints (microfiche), the American Antiquarian Society, Worcester, Mass. Index numbers are 9824, 9825, 20391.

One of the most helpful articles on Sandemanianism in the Colonies was written by Williston Walker. Entitled "The Sandemanians of New England," it was published in the *Annual Report of the American Historical Association, 1901*, (Washington D.C., 1902). Since a very small group of Sandemanians met in Danbury until 1899, Walker had the benefit of proximity of time.

Page 25, **CENTRAL IDEA OF JOHN GLAS**

Walker, "The Sandemanians," 139-140.

Page 26, **NINETEENTH CENTURY CRITIC**

Andrew Fuller, Rev., *The Complete Works of Rev. Andrew Fuller: With a Memoir of His Life,* Vol. II, (Philadelphia: American Baptist Publication Society, 1852), 571.

Page 27, **INTOLERANCE**

Walker, "The Sandemanians," 139.

Page 27 **NOT LAYING UP TREASURES**

Jean F. Hankins reports on the case of Thomas Gold, a prosperous farmer in Redding, a town near Danbury, who became a Sandemanian. He tried to follow its dictates about getting rid of earthly treasure by giving away bushels of wheat, barrels of pork, pounds of sugar and many animals. Afraid that Gold might bankrupt himself and become a public charge, the Redding selectmen appointed an overseer for him. But Gold appealed to the Fairfield Court saying that the overseer "was appointed in order to tie up his hand & prevent him from feeding the hungry and cloathing the naked, especially his despised & afflicted Brethren." There is no record that the court decided the case, but on the outside cover of the original documents was written "Law severe. Not designed to take in such a Case. It appears he acts conscientiously. Charity recommended. A tender Pain. Court will rather Err on the other side." "A Different Kind of Loyalist: The Sandemanians of New England During the Revolutionary War," *New England Quarterly* Vol. LX, 2, (1987): 231.

Page 28, **LOYALTY TO MONARCHY**

In Romans 13:1-7, Paul says "Let every person be subject to the governing authorities. For there is no authority except from God, and those that exist have been instituted by God.

Therefore he who resists the authorities resists what God has appointed, and those who resist will incur judgment. For rulers are not a terror to good conduct, but to bad. Would you have no fear of him who is in authority? Then do what is good and you will receive his approval, for he is God's servant for your good. But if you do wrong, be afraid, for he does not bear the sword in vain; he is the servant of God to execute his wrath on the wrongdoer. Therefore one must be subject, not only to avoid God's wrath but also for the sake of conscience. For the same reason you also pay taxes, for the authorities are ministers of God, attending to this very thing. Pay all of them their dues, taxes to whom taxes are due, revenue to whom revenue is due, respect to whom respect is due, honor to whom honor is due." (Revised Standard Version.)

Page 29, EIGHTEENTH CENTURY THEOLOGY

Robert Sandeman attacked Jonathan Edwards in his *Letters on Theron and Aspasio*. It was Edwards' theology which was of primary importance to the Great Awakening. Of note is the fact that several of the ministers who supported Sandeman in Fairfield County had also supported the Great Awakening. It can be inferred that Sandeman's followers were sympathetic to New Light and Separatist theology or at the very least were somewhat disgruntled with Old Light theology. In the *Annals of the American Pulpit of Commemorative Notices of Distinguished American Clergymen of Various Denominations, Vol. 1*, a minister named John Graham was reported as being active in promoting the Great Awakening along with Rev. Ebenezer White, who would become one of the first supporters of Sandeman, and Daniel Humphreys, who would help form a Sandemanian church in New Haven. William B. Sprague, *Annals of the American Pulpit of Commemorative Notices of Distinguished American Clergymen of Various Denominations, Vol. I*, (New York: Robert Carter & Brothers, 1866), 315. See also Williston Walker, "The Sandemanians of New England," 155.

Page 29, JULIA SMITH AND SANDEMANIANISM

Given the fierce intellectualism of the Smiths, it is paradoxical that they would embrace Sandemanian theology, but both Glas and Sandeman, no matter what they professed, were intellectual and did not shy from deep theological exegesis. It may have been easy to tell a person to accept the "bare work of Jesus Christ without a deed or thought" but making it theologically comprehensible took much mental labor.

Page 30, TWO YALE TUTORS

The two tutors were Richard Woodhull and Ebenezer Russell White, the son of Rev. Ebenezer White. Both men remained Sandemanians, with Russell becoming minister of the Danbury Church and Woodhull becoming a founder of the New Haven church. Woodhull was one of the signers of a letter dated September 14, 1777 explaining to New Haven authorities why Sandemanians felt obliged to remain loyal to the crown, a loyalty which landed them in jail. Dana, *Religious Organizations Collection, Vol. 119*, New Haven Colony Historical Society, 111-113. See also Walker, "The Sandemanians," 152.

Page 30, CONGREGATIONAL CONSOCIATION

The Saybrook Platform of 1708, which was Connecticut's religious constitution, set up two ecclesiastical bodies: consociations of churches and associations of ministers. Organized by counties, they were charged with maintaining order and discipline in the local churches. Oscar Zeichner, *Connecticut's Year's of Controversy: 1750-1776*, (Chapel Hill: Published for the Institute of Early American History and Culture by the University of North Carolina Press, 1949), 11.

Page 30, FALSE DOCTRINE OF WHITE AND TAYLOR

Kingsley, *Contributions*, 299.

Page 31, DEATH OF SANDEMAN

Walker, "The Sandemanians," 155.

Page 31, **TORIES**

> Jean F. Hankins in "A Different Kind of Loyalist," (248)
> concluded that the Sandemanians did not see themselves as
> revolutionaries but as true disciples of Christ. "Some of their
> eighteenth-century contemporaries, however, considered their
> doctrines a threat to pure religion; others thought them a threat
> to social stability. As things turned out, the Sandemanians, as
> loyalists, were never a political danger. Their neighbors,
> misunderstanding the Sandemanians' political stand, treated
> them like all the other Tories -- in some cases, perhaps, just
> a bit worse. The patriots' dislike for the Sandemanians' odd
> religious life probably merged with a dislike for their politics
> at a time when direct attacks on a religious institution or group
> were neither legal nor socially acceptable. So the mob
> wrecking the Portsmouth church, the fearful New Haven
> citizens seeking the exile of the nine or ten Sandemanian
> families there, the militiamen interrogating the Danbury elders
> -- these all may have been displays of religious hostility
> masked behind an acceptable political motive, the protection
> of society from real or supposed enemies in its midst."

Page 32, **NEWTOWN CHURCH**

> Although it is clear that the Newtown Church under Rev.
> Judson was sympathetic to Sandemanianism and that the pulpit
> was vacant for ten years until Zephaniah's arrival, there is the
> implication in some of the records that Zephaniah was himself
> responsible for the church becoming Sandemanian. It is
> possible that there may also have been two congregations in
> Newtown, one a much stricter group than the other. In a letter
> from Edward Foster to Robert Ferrier dated 1782, Foster said
> that the church in Newtown "consisted of eleven men and five
> women and several have since joined them." Walker, "The
> Sandemanians," 157. See also "Fairfield East Association
> Records, Vol.I," "The Fairfield East Consociation Records,"
> Vol.I (1734-1813), and "Historical Sketch and Rules of
> Fairfield East Association and Consociation," (1859), 21,
> which are found in the Archives, United Church of Christ
> Conference Center, Hartford, CT..

Page 32, NEW HAVEN SANDEMANIANS

The New Haven Church was very small including at least among its members Joseph Pynchon, Theophilus Chamberlain, Benjamin Smith, William Richmond, Daniel Humphries, Titus Smith, Richard Woodhull, and Thomas Gold. The two Smiths were from Massachusetts and were not related to Zephaniah. By the time Zephaniah went to Yale, there were probably no Sandemanians left in New Haven, all of them having fled to Halifax, Nova Scotia, and Long Island. Only Richard Woodhull remained following the Revolution.

Page 33, STILES

Stiles, *Diary*, Vol. III, 344.

Page 33, REV. WILDMAN

The quote is from Frances Ellen Burr "Obituary of Julia Smith," March 8, 1886, Smith Papers, Historical Society of Glastonbury.

Mr. Wildman was minister of the Southbury Congregational Church from 1766 to 1812. Interestingly he was "raised up as a minister" in the Danbury Church during the ministry of Rev. Ebenezer White. Kingsley, *Contributions*, 478.

Page 34, QUOTE ON ABANDONMENT OF CHURCH

D. Hamilton Hurd, *History of Fairfield County, Connecticut*, (Philadelphia: J.W. Lewis & Co., 1881), 465.

Page 34, NEWTOWN CHURCH

Although the Newtown Church was totally reorganized in 1799, this was not the end to Sandemanianism. In 1838 John Warner Barber wrote about a small group of Sandemanians who still worshipped in Danbury, Connecticut. "They meet on the Sabbath, and the Thursday afternoon of each week, to exhort and to explain the sacred word. Their church is provided with a large circular table, which occupies nearly half the area of the building, at which the several members seat themselves, each one provided with a copy of the scriptures, and as they individually feel disposed, they read and comment thereon, the females excepted. They appear to worship by themselves, the congregation not partaking therein, being but indifferent spectators of the proceedings. They also add to their former exercises prayer and singing; and after which they assemble at one or the other of the brothers' and sisters' houses, where they partake of a feast." John Warner Barber, *Connecticut Historical Collections*, (New Haven: Durrie & Peck, 1838), 368-69.

Page 35, **SERMON**

Connecticut Conference of Churches Sermon Archives, Hartford, CT.

Page 35, **ZEPHANIAH AS REBEL**

Asa Smith, Zephaniah's younger brother, broke off from the Eastbury Congregational Church in 1796 and helped form the first Methodist Church in town. This indicates that the spirit of religious dissent was not confined to the older brother. Methodism was viewed with deep dismay by many Congregationalists. According to Purcell, "To the minister of the Standing Order, the untutored exhorter fresh from the shop or field was a demagogue ranting the Word of God. The Methodist ministry, if possible, was even more primitive than that in which the Baptist gloried. Their large, often unauthorized camp meetings were the source of much annoyance; for Connecticut was not in favor of anything but the most orderly, godly revival; and many a minister questioned the propriety of any revival." Richard J. Purcell, *Connecticut in Transition: 1775-1818*, (Middletown, CT.: Wesleyan University Press, 1963), 58.

Most of Zephaniah's family moved to New York State, Ohio, and Indiana early in the nineteenth century, including his mother Ruth Hollister Smith who moved to New York State. His father Isaac died in 1796 in Glastonbury. On February 1, 1815 Julia wrote in her diary "In the afternoon Father's two

sisters and his brother-in-law and one of his nephews came
here from Granville of New York State. It is fourteen years
since I have seen them. We were very glad to see them."
Smith Papers, Historical Society of Glastonbury.

Page 36, JONATHAN BRACE

Purcell, *Connecticut in Transition*, 129, 132.

Page 37, INFLUENCE ON DAUGHTERS

In her study of intellectual women in America from 1830 to
1860, Susan Conrad notes that law was the most common
profession of the fathers. (Elizabeth Cady Stanton, the Grimke
sisters, and Margaret Fuller all had fathers who were lawyers
to name a few.) "The response of women intellectuals to the
idea of opportunity was modeled upon the professional
orientations and ideals they had absorbed from their fathers.
America's first generation of intellectual women all discovered
that some form of intellectual activity was the only way they
could live up to these ideals of learned excellence and ability,
the only way to unite their experience as Americans with the
cultural definitions of the American woman and her sphere."
Susan Conrad, *Perish the Thought: Intellectual Women in
Romantic America, 1830-1860*, (Secaucas, N.J.: The Citadel
Press, 1978), 175.

CHAPTER 3 -- THE EARLY YEARS

Page 38, SALE OF FARM

Lillian E. Prudden, "Memoirs," 1949, Mss., Smith Papers,
Historical Society of Glastonbury, 10.

Page 39, HANCY ZEPHINA

The name Hancy appears as Handsa in the early letters,
however, the name was rarely used. She herself wrote her
name H. Zephina. Occasionally, the spelling Zephine with the

letter "e" appears.

Page 40, **QUOTE OF JULIA**

Prudden, "Memoirs," 4.

Page 40, **LETTER FROM HANNAH**

This entry presents a problem of dates. Abby Hadassah was born June 1, 1797, but this letter seems to be dated 1796, yet Hannah refers to five girls with the last just being weaned which means the letter should be dated 1798 at the earliest. Smith Papers, Connecticut State Library, Hartford, CT..

Page 41, **HANNAH'S INVOLVEMENT WITH FARM**

Some of the second-hand accounts state that Hannah was frail and that one of the reasons the Smiths moved from South Britain to Glastonbury was because her "health could no longer endure the unaccustomed work of a farm," yet Hannah's own diary belies that statement. She remained active on the Smith farm until the end of her life.

Page 41, **ACCOUNT BOOK**

Cott, *The Bonds of Womanhood*, 43-44.

Page 42, **MEMBERS OF THE SMITH HOUSEHOLD**

During the 1820s, there was also a boy named Joseph Minor living with the Smiths. He was apparently an orphan who was placed with the Smiths by the Town of Glastonbury.

Page 42, **LETTER FROM ZEPHANIAH**

Smith Papers, Historical Society of Glastonbury.

Page 43, **POEM**

Hannah Smith, *Mother's Poems*, (Published by Julia Smith,

1881), Historical Society of Glastonbury.

Page 44, **LETTER**

Smith Papers, Historical Society of Glastonbury.

Page 45, **THE HARTFORD COURANT**

Smith Papers, Historical Society of Glastonbury.

Page 46, **WOMAN OF LETTERS**

Conrad, *Perish the Thought*, 184-185.

Page 47, **ASTRONOMY AND POETRY**

Mother's Poems, Introduction.

Page 49, **JULIA'S ILLNESS**

The letter is actually dated February 1813, but Julia's diary shows that she was very ill for six weeks in February 1812. After being ill several times in January, Julia last wrote in her diary on February 4 and did not write again until March 21 when she wrote "I have been sick for six weeks. I have been very ill. Grandfather and Grandmother came here February 29th. I have not been outside the house yet. Dr. Reed has been here almost every day until this week." Letter, Smith Papers, Connecticut State Library. Diary, Connecticut Historical Society.

Page 50, **LATIN GRAMMAR**

J.H. Hale, "The Famous Smith Family of Glastonbury, Connecticut," Mss, Smith Papers, Historical Society of Glastonbury, undated, 3. Prudden, "Memoirs," 5.

Page 50, **MARRIAGE**

On November 5, 1811, Julia noted in her diary that a marriage had been performed in her father's office.

CHAPTER 4 -- SISTERHOOD/SPINSTERHOOD

Page 54, **SKETCHES**

Anon, cited in Cott, *The Bonds of Womanhood*, 110.

Page 55, **SARAH PIERCE QUOTE**

Helen M. Sheldrick, *Pioneer Women Teachers of Connecticut*, (Winsted, CT: Dowd Printing Company, 1971), 6.

Page 56, **LETTER FROM ABBY**

Smith Papers, Connecticut State Library.

Pg. 56, **VALUE**

Phyllis Kihn, "The Value Family of Connecticut," *The Connecticut Historical Society Bulletin*, 34, no.3 (July), 79-93.

Page. 61, **OLCUTT**

Julia Smith diary, November 26, 1823, December 25, 1823.

Pg. 61, **COTT**

Cott, *The Bonds of Womanhood*, 177.

Pg. 61, **FRIENDSHIP WITH BEECHERS**

Familiarity, if not friendship, between the Smiths and the Beechers would have been natural, given the fact that both families were involved in similar causes: women's education, women's rights, and abolition. However, neither the Stowe-Day Foundation nor the Connecticut Historical Society, both in Hartford, Connecticut, have any evidence that Laurilla taught at Catherine Beecher's school nor any other reference which would link the families during this time period. During their involvement in the suffrage movement beginning in the late 1860s, Julia and Abby became friends with Isabella Beecher Hooker who was born in 1822. The other female friend of note in the area was Lydia Huntley Sigourney, the "sweet singer of Hartford."

Page 62, **ROMANTIC INTERESTS**

In an undated manuscript written many years after the death of Julia by Florence Hollister Curtis of Glastonbury, she relates that the sisters sometimes played games with a suitor, making up rhymes between them, hinting that it was time for him to leave, hints he was too obtuse to grasp. The Historical Society of Glastonbury.

Page 63, **ZEPHANIAH AND MARRIAGE**

There is no evidence that Zephaniah withheld opportunities for company in any way. In fact, the daughters had a very full social life.

Page 64, **PRUDDEN QUOTE**

Lillian Prudden was the great-great-granddaughter of Eleazer Mitchel whose second wife was Abigail Hickok Mitchel, the mother of Hannah. (The name "Mitchel" is spelled with one or two letter "l's".) In her memoir, she said that "the Mitchell homestead situated in that part of Ancient Woodbury bordering on the Housatonic river called South Britain, was always hospitably opened to both sets of grandchildren with the result that the 'Glastenbury [sic] Smiths' were always called 'Cousin' by the Mitchells and there was visiting back and forth." Lillian Prudden was a little girl when the Smiths were elderly. Her memoir is most reliable when she relates her own personal recollections of the family in the 1870s. Mss., Historical Society of Glastonbury, 1949, pg. 1.

Page 65, **HUNT**

Katherine Hunt was the granddaughter of Hulda Hollister, the sister of Ruth Hollister, who was Zephaniah's mother. Her journal is in the Henry Whitfield State Historical Museum, Guilford, Ct.

Page 66, **WELLES QUOTE**

> Henry Titus Welles grew up on Main Street not far from the
> Smiths. As had Katherine Hunt, he also stayed in touch with
> the family even after he moved out of Glastonbury. He stated
> in his book that "Mrs. Parker went from Hartford to
> Washington, to attend a women's convention, in 1880, and
> returned alone. She stopped at my house in New York a day
> or two." Parker was Julia Smith's married name. Henry Titus
> Welles, *Autobiography and Reminiscences. Vol.I,*
> (Minneapolis: Marshall Robinson, 1899), 84.

Page 66, **PAINTING**

> The painting of Zephaniah is owned by the Springfield
> Museum of Fine Arts in Springfield, Massachusetts.

Page 67, **NEWSPAPER ARTICLE**

> The undated newspaper article, entitled "Two 18th Century
> 'New Women,' The Smith Sisters' Portraits," was written by
> Ella J. Harris for the *Sunday Republican*. Smith Papers,
> Historical Society of Glastonbury.

CHAPTER 5 -- RELIGION: THE WAY OF THE JUST

Page 70, **DE TOCQUEVILLE**

> Alexis deTocqueville, ed. by John Stone and Stephen Mennell,
> *On Democracy, Revolutions and Society: Selected Writings,*
> (Chicago and London: The University of Chicago Press,
> 1980), Part 1, Chapter 17, 89.

Page. 71, **PROOF-TEXTING**

> In one typical example, a character in the book *Northwood or,*
> *Life North and South*, by Sarah Josepha Hale (published in
> 1852), decries some of the evils which had arisen in
> conjunction with slavery but declared it to be scripturally

acceptable, "but as this particular institution was allowed and regulated by the authority of God among His chosen people, it could not, at that time, have been a sin to be condemned." (1852, reprinted 1972:395). Just as religion condoned slavery, so religion was also the answer to the problems it presented. "Instructed in Christianity the slave on earth has the key of heavenly freedom; and the one who is really a Christian should bless God for the privileges that American slavery has conferred on himself and on his race." (Freeport, New York: Books for Libraries, 1972), 395, 400.

Page 71, **HENRY CLAY**

Appendix to the <u>Congressional Globe</u>, Dec. 1838: 358.

Page 71, **SEARCH FOR A MINISTER**

Smith Papers, Letter to Abigail Mitchell, Connecticut State Library.

At the end of her life, Julia sometimes told reporters that her family had never belonged to any church. Unfortunately, the First Church (also called the First Society) membership records for the early nineteenth century cannot be used for verification because they are not complete. However, the diary and the early letters make clear that the Smiths did attend. By the time Julia and Abby were involved with suffrage they sometimes slanted their early history when speaking with reporters to bring it into line with their present thinking. The part that the established church played in their youth was one such area which was slanted.

Page 73, **AWAKENING IN GLASTONBURY**

Prince Hawes was minister of the First Society. The Methodist Church had been established in Glastonbury in 1796. Alonza B. Chapin, *Glastenbury [sic] for Two Hundred Years 1853*, (Hartford: Press of Case, Tiffany and Co., 1853, Reprinted by the Historical Society of Glastonbury, 1976), 146. A part of what is called the Second Great Awakening, this type of religious excitement was intermittent in Glastonbury.

Page 75, MILLERISM

It is unclear whether all the Smiths were involved in Millerism or only Julia and Abby.

In 1 Thessalonians 4:16-18 Paul said "For the Lord himself will descend from the heaven with a cry of command, with the archangel's call and with the sound of the trumpet of God: and the dead in Christ will rise first; then we who are alive, who are left, shall be caught up together with them in the clouds to meet the Lord in the air; and so we shall always be with the Lord. Therefore comfort one another with these words."

Page 75, OCTOBER 22, 1844

Miller himself did not want to predict a precise date and hour. The October 22, 1844 date was chosen by some of his fellow leaders based on the Day of Atonement, the tenth day of the seventh month. Pressured to endorse the date, Miller finally did so wholeheartedly, declaring "Thank the Lord. I am almost home. Glory! Glory! Glory!." David L. Rowe, *Thunder and Trumpets: Millerites and Dissenting Religions in Upstate New York, 1800-1850*, (Chico, California: Scholars Press, 1985), 135-136.

Page 75, MILLER QUOTE

This quote is taken from a letter written by William Miller to Elder Hendryx dated May 20, 1832. Clara Endicott Sears, *Days of Delusion: A Strange Bit of History*, (Boston and New York: Houghton Mifflin Company, The Riverside Press, 1924), 35-36.

Page 76, ROWE QUOTE

Rowe, *Thunder and Trumpets*, 4.

Page 77, JOSEPH WRIGHT

Diary, Historical Society of Glastonbury.

Page 78, ZEPHANIAH SMITH SERMON

Connecticut Conference of Churches Sermon Archives, Hartford, CT.

Page 79, SEVENTH DAY ADVENTIST CHURCH

Out of the ashes of the Great Disappointment would arise the Seventh-Day Adventist Church. In order to establish a permanent group, the Millerites had to reassess the idea of the Second Coming being imminent. Jonathan Butler in his article "The Making of a New Order," says "The key to transforming an effervescent apocalypticism into an established, complex religious system includes, above all, an elongation of the eschatological timetable. As long as a group sustains short-term, specific predictions of the end it remains volatile. With each passing of a prophetic date, conversions vaporize into apostasies, the promised harvest results in crop failure. The sooner the group can shed its short-term millenarianism, the sooner it can accommodate to the practical business of living life in the world." For the Seventh-Day Adventists, the answer was to see October 22, 1844 as the date when an investigation of sin had begun in preparation for the end of the world. Jonathan Butler, In *The Disappointed*, eds. Ronald L. Numbers and Jonathan M. Butler, (Bloomington and Indianapolis: Indiana University Press, 1987), 200.

Page 79, HENRY TITUS WELLES

Welles, *Autobiography,* 84.

Page 79, MARY T. HALE

Undated manuscript, Historical Society of Glastonbury.

Page 79, ASCENSION ROBES

The issue of whether there were actually ascension robes is a sensitive one for Seventh-Day Adventists. The Biblical impetus came from Revelation Chapter 6 and 7 which describes crowds of believers robed in white. There are many accounts of people having ascension robes in readiness for the coming of Christ, but often the accounts are second-hand, as is the case with the Smiths. Part of the reason for the focus on the robes by the press was that they seemed to sum up for non-believers the extreme credulity of people who thought the world was coming to an abrupt end.

Page 79, **MILLER'S DISAPPOINTMENT**

Wayne R. Judd, "William Miller, Disappointed Prophet," in *The Disappointed*, eds. Ronald L. Numbers and Jonathan M. Butler, (Bloomington and Indianapolis: Indiana University Press, 1987), 20.

Page 81, **JARVIS**

Jarvis is mentioned as the man who encouraged Julia to learn Hebrew in the memoir written by Mrs. J.H. Hale, owned by the Historical Society of Glastonbury. Lillian Prudden in her memoir mentions a Judge Thayer of Middletown. There is a very small book in the Historical Society of Glastonbury called *Gift of Piety or Divine Breathings in One Hundred Meditations* which has a hand-written inscription to Julia from E.A. Thayer, but E.A. Thayer was a Hartford physician and not a Middletown judge.

Apart from the fact that Samuel Jarvis was a Biblical scholar and Bible collector, there is another reason why he was probably the person who encouraged Julia to study Hebrew: he himself had attempted to check the accuracy of Miller's arithmetic and had pointed out that Miller's addition did not agree with that done by Bishop James Ussher who had determined that the world began in 4004 B.C. Although it is only conjecture, Julia may have contacted Samuel Jarvis upon reading his disputation. Doan, *The Disappointed*, 123-125.

For full information on Jarvis and his library, see **Wyman W. Parker**, "The Jarvis Library," *Serif*, No. 2, 1964.

Page 81, **TRANSLATION**

> *Hartford Daily Times*, December 11, 1875, Historical Society of Glastonbury.

Page 82, **ABBY'S INFLUENCE**

> In a letter from Abby Smith to C.C. Burleigh September 9, 1862, she refers to the Bible as "our Bible." Other correspondence reveals that Abby was deeply involved in spreading and defending the idea that the scripture was sufficient to bring a person to a knowledge of God without the aid of ministers or Bible commentaries. Writing to Dr. Pinckney W. Ellsworth, a Hartford physician, on April 24, 1866, Abby congratulated him on his personal search of the Scriptures. "Most men of deep & investigating minds, especially of your profession, seeing the inconsistency of many of the doctrines promulgated by the clergy, have discarded the bible, believing that book sanctions such doctrines, without searching it to see for themselves. But there is no understanding it unless we do search for ourselves, each one, as we would for hid treasures." Smith Papers, Historical Society of Glastonbury.

Page 82, **QUOTE FROM JULIA**

> Smith, *The Holy Bible*, Preface.

Page 82, **WRIGHT DIARY**

> Diary, Historical Society of Glastonbury.

Page 84, **BIBLE**

> In 2 Corinthians 3:4-6 Paul says "And such trust have we though Christ to God-ward: Not that we are sufficient of ourselves to think any thing as of ourselves; but our sufficiency is of God. Who also hath made us able [sufficient as] ministers of the new testament; not of the letter, but of the spirit; for the letter killeth, but the spirit giveth life. (King James Version)

Page 87, **FREDERICK C. GRANT**

> Frederick C. Grant, *Translating the Bible*, (Greenwich, Ct: Seabury Press, 1961), 88.

Page 88, **BURR**

> Elizabeth Cady Stanton, *The Woman's Bible*, 1898 (Coalition Task Force on Women and Religion, reprint 1986), 149.

Page 89, **SMITH-ROSENBERG**

> Carroll Smith-Rosenberg, *Disorderly Conduct*, (New York and Oxford: Oxford University Press, 1985), 129.

Page 91, **GRAYBILL**

> Graybill, *The Disappointed*, 145-146.

CHAPTER 6 -- THE CULTURAL ROOTS OF ABOLITIONISM

Page 93, **DONALD**

> In some ways Donald's thesis borrowed from Avery Craven's thesis that abolitionists were motivated by economic and social upheavals in the North; therefore, the real reason for the Civil War according to Craven (but not according to Donald) was the "inflamed imagination [of the abolitionists] which endowed the institution [of slavery] with all the ills possible in its theory and assigned to the slave-owner all the qualities and characteristics desirable in a bitter rival." David Donald, *Lincoln Reconsidered*, (New York: Vintage Books, 1961), 22, 36. Avery Craven cited in Weisberger, *Abolition: Disrupter of the Democratic System or Agent of Progress?*, (Chicago: Rand McNally & Co., 1963), 5.

Page 94, **ANTI-SLAVERY PETITIONS**

> All drafts of the Smiths' anti-slavery petitions are in the Smith

Papers, Historical Society of Glastonbury.

Page 95, MAGDOL

Edward Magdol, *The Anti-Slavery Rank and File, A Social Profile of the Abolitionists' Constituency*, (New York, Westport, CT, London: Greenwood Press, 1986), 60.

Page 97, PECULIAR INSTITUTION

The Revisionist theory as put forth by Avery Craven and James G. Randell stated that the Civil War was needless because slavery was withering away. That being the case, abolition was really a break-down in the democratic process of discussion. But research since then by many historians including Kenneth M. Stampp (1956) and Eugene Genovese (1972) has shown that the opposite was true. Craven and Randell cited in Weisberger, *Abolition: Disrupter of the Democratic System*, 5.

Page 98, NATURE OF SLAVERY

Stampp, *The Peculiar Institution*, 28.

Page 98, PLANTATION

Eugene D. Genovese defines a plantation as a unit of 20 or more slaves, which would mean that half the slaves lived on farms. However, Stampp contends that well over half were on plantation units of more than 20, and one-fourth were in units of more than 50 (1956: 31). Genovese, *Roll, Jordon, Roll: The World The Slaves Made*, (New York: Vintage Books, 1972, ed. 1976), 7. Kenneth M. Stampp, *The Peculiar Institution: Slavery in the Ante-Bellum South*, (New York: Vintage Books, 1956,

Page 98, CRUELTY

Stampp, *The Peculiar Institution*, 185.

Page 99, **LETTER**

Smith Papers, Connecticut State Library.

Page 99, **SPINNING**

According to Nancy Cott, the mills changed women's lives more than any other single factor in the early nineteenth century. Spinning and weaving were essential parts of farm life. With those tasks taken over by mills, the work that women performed became more marginal economically. The result was that women were perceived as more marginal, which led to an idealization of women as physically frail and incapable of performing hard work. *The Bonds of Womanhood*, 20, 36.

Page 99, **JOHN QUINCY ADAMS**

Adams cited in Barbara J. Berg, *The Remembered Gate: Origins of American Feminism: The Woman and the City, 1800-1860*, (New York: Oxford University Press, 1978), 32.

Page 100, **AFRICAN DESCENT**

The Smiths used the terms "Negro," "people of color" and "colored" in their diaries and petitions. In this paper, the term used principally is "Negro."

Page 101, **QUOTE**

This quote was translated by Mary Helen Kidder and is undated in her manuscript (1937, 9). Connecticut Historical Society.

Page 102, **WEBBER**

Webber cites Norman R. Yetman, ed., Life Under the "Peculiar Institution": Selections from the Slave Narrative Collection (New York: Holt, Rinehart and Winston, 1970), 52. Thomas L. Webber, *Deep Like The Rivers: Education in the Slave Quarter Community, 1831-1865*, (New York and

London: W.W. Norton & Co., 1978), 47.

Page 103, **BUYING FREEDOM**

Gwendolyne Evans Logan "The Slave in Connecticut During the American Revolution," in *Connecticut Historical Society Bulletin*, 30, No. 3: 73-80.

Page 106, **COMMITMENT**

They were also deeply suspicious of Southern politicians, a suspicion which in Hannah's and Zephaniah's case probably stretched back to the Constitutional Convention. This suspicion may have been underscored by the Hartford Convention of 1814 in which Federalists, such as Zephaniah, called for the elimination of the Three-fifths Rule. Zephaniah was in Hartford, supposedly for court cases, for the entire period of the Hartford Convention which was held in November 1814, but there is no way to determine whether he attended as an observer. Paradoxically, and confusingly, two of the delegates from Connecticut were Zephaniah Swift and Nathaniel Smith, men whom Zephaniah knew well.

CHAPTER 7 -- THE ANTI-SLAVERY PETITIONS

Page 109, **CRANDELL**

Prudence Crandall attempted to teach black girls, some from out of state, at her school in Canterbury, Connecticut, beginning in 1831. Incensed, the residents of Canterbury smashed windows, fouled her drinking water, and taunted her and her students. In May 1833 the Connecticut legislature passed a law making it illegal to educate black students from out-of-state without the consent of local town governments. Prudence Crandall refused to obey and was arrested. Her subsequent conviction was overturned by a higher court, but when she bravely returned to Canterbury and reopened her school, she faced mob violence. Forced to close the school, she moved with her husband to Illinois and then to Kansas.

Elihu Burritt gained fame by developing an international coalition which pushed for a peaceful settlement of the Oregon boundary dispute in 1846. Richard Rust was living in Middletown, Connecticut, at the time the Smiths knew him, having come from Wilbraham Academy in Massachusetts to Wesleyan. Julia considered him a highly talented, unique individual.

Page 109, INFERIORITY

Winthrop D. Jordan in *White Over Black: American Attitudes Toward the Negro, 1550-1812* wrote about the paradoxical attitude of many whites toward blacks. "Within every white American who stood confronted by the Negro, there had arisen a perpetual duel between his higher and lower natures. His cultural conscience -- his Christianity, his humanitarianism, his ideology of liberty and equality -- demanded that he regard and treat the Negro as his brother and his countryman, as his equal. At the same moment, however, many of his most profound urges, especially his yearning to maintain the identity of his folk, his passion for domination, his sheer avarice, and his sexual desire, impelled him toward conceiving and treating the Negro as inferior to himself, as an American leper. At closer view, though, the duel appears more complex than a conflict between the best and worst in the white man's nature, for in a variety of ways the white man translated his "worst" into his "best." Raw sexual aggression became retention of purity, and brutal domination became faithful maintenance of civilized restraints. These translations, so necessary to the white man's peace of mind, were achieved at devastating cost to another people set permanently apart because they looked different from the white man generation after generation." (New York, London: W. W. Norton & Co., 1968), 581-582.

Page 110, PETITION DRIVE

Magdol, *The Anti-Slavery Rank and File*, 54.

Page 110, **WAYLAND**

> Wayland's book *The Limitations of Human Responsibility* was published in Boston in 1838 by the publishing firm of Gould, Kendell and Lincoln. The section which received the most criticism was Section 9 entitled "The Slavery Question" from which this quote is taken. William Henry Smith (no relation of the Smiths) wrote a book or tract called *A Review of That Portion of the 9th Section of President Wayland's Valuable Treatise on the Limitations of Human Responsibility* which was published in 1840.

Page 110, **RACIAL INFERIORITY**

> The idea of racial inferiority was clearly expressed by Willbur Fisk, President of Wesleyan College and a leader of the African Colonization Movement in Connecticut. In 1834 he said "The greatest and almost the only disability of the free colored people, in this country are resolvable into what has been called the prejudice of color. In combatting this prejudice, the first inquiry should be, is it vincible or invincible? Does it exist, in nature, or is it the effect merely of education and casual association? I am prepared to say...that in my opinion, it is to a certain extent natural and invincible...Our instincts, physical and moral, act independently of reasoning; and they dictate at once, that anything like a social or domestic equality between races can never be enjoyed. " David E. Swift, *Sense of Mission, White and Black, in the Jacksonian Era: Willbur Fisk and Charles Ray*, Mss, Archives, Olin Library, Wesleyan University, Middletown, Ct, 207.

Page 114, **JEFFERSON**

> Jordan, *White Over Black*, 547.

Page 117, **GARRISON**

> Cited in Aileen Kraditor, *Means and Ends in American Abolition*, (New York: Pantheon Books, 1967), 85.

CHAPTER 8 -- THE PROBLEM OF POLITICAL POWERLESSNESS

Page 120, **FREE SPEECH**

Smith Papers, Historical Society of Glastonbury.

Page 120, **CONGRESSIONAL PETITIONS**

Magdol, *The Anti-Slavery Rank and File*, 54.

Page 120, **JOHN QUINCY ADAMS**

Leonard L. Richards, "The Jacksonians and Slavery," in *Antislavery Reconsidered: New Perspectives on the Abolitionists*, (Baton Rouge and London: Louisiana State University Press, 1979), 110.

Oddly Adams for all his eloquence and dogged support, did not consider himself an abolitionist.

Page 122, **GAG RULE**

William W. Freehling in his book *The Road to Disunion: Secessionists at Bay, 1776-1854 Volume I* provides a different explanation for the dismay of northerners at the gag rule. Although not fanatical about liberty for blacks, they considered "egalitarian republicanism for whites" to be sacred. "Sacred. That word lay behind Charles Grandison Finney's preaching and Theodore Dwight Weld's crusade. But few Yankees thought blacks' rights to liberty so sacred as to cause a holy war with righteous Southerners. Whites' democratic rights, on the other hand, were as precious as the sacrament." (New York: Oxford University Press, 1990), 294.

Page 123, **DIARY ENTRY**

Hannah Smith, 1848, Connecticut State Library, 95.

Page 124, **WILMOT PROVISO**

> The Wilmot Proviso was continually resubmitted to Congress up until the Compromise of 1850. Congressman Abraham Lincoln of Illinois voted for it more than 40 times.

Page 125, **UNDERGROUND RAILROAD**

> In his book *The Underground Railroad in Connecticut*, Horatio T. Strother stated that the Smiths were part of the underground railroad on the basis of the fact that they were strong abolitionists. However, this assumption is not justified; although all underground railroaders were abolitionists, not all abolitionists were underground railroaders. (Middletown, Ct: Wesleyan University Press, 1961), 139.

Page 126, **BEMAN**

> Beman Papers, Beineke Library Yale University.

> The convention to which Hannah referred was probably a meeting of the Colored Men of the State of Connecticut, of which the Bemans were members and officers.

Page 128, **DEATH OF HANNAH**

> Wright Diary, report of weather, Historical Society of Glastonbury, Dec 27, 1850.

Page 128, **LETTER**

> Smith Papers, Letter to Mr. Cothren, Historical Society of Glastonbury.

Page 129, **EVERY SEVEN YEARS**

> Smith Papers, "Two 18th Century 'New Women,'" undated, Historical Society of Glastonbury.

Page 130, **LETTER FROM ABBY**

Smith Papers, Historical Society of Glastonbury.

Page 131, **FEAR FOR COUNTRY**

Smith Papers, Historical Society of Glastonbury.

Gideon Welles, Secretary of the Navy, was born in Glastonbury in 1802. Along with the Smiths, the Welles family were leaders in town. The Smiths were close with certain branches of the family.

Page 131, **TREATMENT OF BLACKS**

Letter from Abby Smith to Mr. R.J. Moffatt, Smith Papers, Historical Society of Glastonbury.

Page 132, **WATER CURE**

Copies of the magazine *The Water Cure*, which belonged to the Smiths, are owned by the Historical Society of Glastonbury.

Page 133, **LETTER**

Smith Papers, Letter to Mrs. Demarise, Historical Society of Glastonbury.

CHAPTER 9 -- RESOUNDING THE BATTLE CRY

Page 134, **ABBY SMITH AND HER COWS**

The sale of *Abby Smith and Her Cows*, published in 1876, spread the word about woman suffrage far and wide while helping offset the sisters' legal fees. All of the recent articles which have been published on the Smiths' tax battle with the Town of Glastonbury have relied almost exclusively on this book. Although it is extremely useful, the clapbook does not present a balanced picture. Julia did not include clippings in support of the town's position or which presented a positive image of the tax collector and the town officials.

Page 135, PASTORAL LETTER

Kraditor, *Means and Ends in American Abolition*, 43, 45.

Page 136, LETTER TO KELLEY

Kelley Papers, American Antiquarian Society, Worcester, Massachusetts.

Page 137, UNIVERSAL SUFFRAGE

According to Barbara Berg, the extension of suffrage, "as it brought in new votes, carried new men into politics also. Since they lacked prior experience in public affairs, these newcomers developed their own tactics and ethics in the vote-getting arena. Pragmatic, opportunistic, and often ruthless, these novices accomplished significant change in the nature of American politics. First and most apparent, the well-bred elites who had previously been dominant were slowly pushed from the scene." *The Remembered Gate*, 32.

Page 137, DUBOIS

Dubois, eds. Michael Fellman and Lewis Perry, *Antislavery Reconsidered*, 241.

Page 137, DECISION TO GO TO CONVENTION

Smith, *Abby Smith and Her Cows*, intro..

Page 139, ANTHONY

The Hartford Courant, October 29, 1869.

Page 139, TRUTH ON THEIR SIDE

Smith, *Abby Smith and Her Cows*, intro.

Page 140, **BOUND BY NO LAW**

Ibid., 34.

Page 140, **DEATH OF ZEPHINA**

Ibid., intro.

Page 141, **ABBY'S RESPONSE**

Ibid., intro.

Page 141, **ROSELLA BUCKINGHAM**

Rosella Buckingham died in South Glastonbury on March 23, 1875 at the age of 42. Julia wrote "She was probably the most beautiful as well as the most talented woman ever reared in Glastonbury. She exerted herself in the cause of Woman Suffrage until her health gave out, and for nearly a year she was mostly confined to her bed by distressing illness. Her articles, published in the journals of the day, were powerful specimens of intellectual effort, and were inserted in many of the newspapers of Hartford, Springfield, Boston, Providence, Chicago, Washington, &c. The Suffrage cause has lost an able advocate and friend, and society one of its brightest ornaments" (Ibid., 52). The following letter (excerpted), titled "Which is Highest, Law or Justice?", which Rosella Buckingham wrote to *The Hartford Daily Times*, dated January 14, 1874, was reprinted in *Abby Smith and Her Cows*:

"December 16, 1773, a party of men, disguised as Indians, went on board some vessels in Boston Harbor, and threw their cargoes overboard. No one ever claimed that the act was in accordance with law, but it has been cited as an instance where man's love of justice overcame his respect for law. Now, may I ask, how the action of the Misses Smith, in refusing to submit to being taxed without being represented, differs, in spirit, from that of 1773, which has been highly commended? If "Resistance to tyrants is obedience to God," why is it not as honorable for a woman to resist injustice, in her own chosen way, as it is for a man? There is no question of minors or idiots in this, but one of woman's right to self-government; and why men should fear to grant that right which they consider their highest privilege, to women, while declaring that not one woman in five hundred would exercise her right to the franchise, is a mystery. If the suffrage should bring upon women all the evils which men predict, are women so devoid of wit as to retain a right which has proved injurious to them? Why not tell the truth? Say, "We want our slaves to remain as they are, forever." You will never do that. Men prefer to cry "Great is Diana of the Ephesians," when the secret thought of their hearts is, "Our craft is in danger." So you cry up "law and order," while dooming others, in no way inferior to yourselves, to a life that no law would make you endure for one year..."

Page 141, SELECTMENS' MEETING

The records of selectmens' meetings and the electors' meetings of the Town of Glastonbury for this period list the attendees, people running for office and elected, and issues voted upon by the committeemen. Business on which no joint action was necessary was generally not recorded.

Page 143, PRUDDEN

Lillian Prudden wrote that the increase in visits was made possible because her "mother had proved herself advanced enough to have me go to college and particularly after my brother Henry courteously escorted Julia and Abby to a large suffrage meeting where he helped them to the seats on the platform to which they were invited." Prior to that, the relationship had always been cordial but a little distant because Prudden's father was a minister, "but the fact that my father was firm in an anti-slavery position when it cost something to withstand the pressure, mitigated in later years the odium of being the family of a "hireling priest." Memoirs, 1949, 12-13, Historical Society of Glastonbury.

Page 144, TEMPEST IN TEAPOT

Smith, *Abby Smith and Her Cows*, 18,10.

Page 145, **UNSAFE FROM MEN**

> Ibid., 9,9,10,11,22.

Page 146, **NEWSPAPER ARTICLES**

> Ibid., 9.

Page 148, **COWS**

> Ibid., 38, 13.

Page 149, **BOSTON TEA PARTY COMPARISON**

> Ibid., 14.

Page 150, **AUCTION**

> Ibid., 14.

Page 151, **CHARITY**

> Ibid., 24.

Page 151, **VALUE OF ESTATE**

> Pamela Cartledge, "Seven Cows On The Auction Block: Abby and Julia Smith's Fight for Enfranchisement of Women," *The Connecticut Historical Society Bulletin*, 52, No.1 (1987, Winter): 22.

CHAPTER 10 -- NATIONAL ATTENTION AND LOCAL ANTAGONISM

Page 153, **ISABELLA BEECHER HOOKER QUOTE**

> J. Smith, *Abby Smith and Her Cows*, 18.

Page 153, **WOMAN SUFFRAGE RESOLUTIONS**

The following resolution passed at the Rhode Island Suffrage Association in January 1874 is typical of many resolutions passed during this period. "Resolved. That we heartily approve the noble stand for principle taken by Miss Abby Smith and her sister of Glastonbury, Conn., in refusing to pay taxes for the support of a government, which denies their representation without just cause. Resolved. That we sympathize with them in the persecution which has followed their act, while at the same time we welcome them to the honorable company, whose praises have so recently been sung at "tea parties" all over the land -- of those who dare offer assistance to tyranny, by <u>deeds</u> as well as <u>words</u>: and that we hope and believe their example will be followed by others, until our laggard legislators are scourged to their duty in regard to woman, by the whip of a public sentiment which tolerates no injustice. Anna C. Garlin, Cor. Sec. R.I.W.S.A., Mrs. Elizabeth Chace, President, Mrs. Louis J. Doyle, Char. Ex. Com."

Page 153, **AUCTION OF COWS**

The following poem was written by an anonymous correspondent from Boston:

<u>The Drum of Glastonbury</u>

The brave boys of Connecticut
     Went marching to the fight;
Beating their drums they onward strode
     To battle day and night.

They fought to keep the nation free;
     "The Union" was their cry;
Our fathers won us liberty
     And shall our country die?

What proud procession passes on?
     Why sounds the drum to-day?

Why to the sigh-post through the town,
        Do people take their way?

Who answers to the roll-call now?
        Those seven cows, you see,
And forty men with rush to buy
        These cows -- for liberty.

The drum that beat ten years ago
        To rebels -- Right is Might,
Now wakens echoes round our homes
        That answer -- Might is Right.

We choose to tax Miss Abby Smith
        To say we shall not vote;
The cows we now put up for sale
        Our liberties denote.

Oh! brave boys of Connecticut,
        Beat loudly your battle drum;
To auction block of liberty
        Bid all your men now come.

Page 153, BOUQUETS OF FLOWERS

The bouquets were made by Emma V. Hallet who had visited
the Smiths and, as reported in the *Hartford Times*, "divested
the cows' tails of sufficient hair for this purpose, presenting
one of the bouquets to Miss Smith and the other to the Bazaar.
The original number of these celebrated Alderneys was seven.
Two have been sold, so five are represented in the bouquet.
The hair of Jessy, the grandmother of the flock, is made into
a jasmine. Daisy and Minney are her children, and the hair of
Daisy being of a suitable color, forms a bunch of daisies, the
resemblance being complete. Roxey and Whitey are Jessy's
grandchildren, Roxey's hair being made into cowslips, and
Whitey's into buttercups -- cowslips and buttercups -- names
very fitting for the occasion, and the flowers very beautifully
made..." J. Smith, *Abby Smith and Her Cows*, 43.

Page 154, **GARRISON**

Ibid., 29.

Page 155, **SPEECH BY ABBY**

Ibid., 32.

Page 156, **ABBY AND ROAD WORK**

Ibid., 34.

Page 157, **HARTFORD WEEKLY TIMES**

Smith Papers, Historical Society of Glastonbury.

Page 159, **SALE OF LAND**

J. Smith, *Abby Smith and Her Cows*, 43.

Page 161, **DESCRIPTION OF TRIAL**

Ibid., 45-46.

Page 164, **TINKERING WITH JUDICIAL SYSTEM**

Julia and Abby contended that George G. Sumner was not the regular judge who they had been told was sick. Writing to the *Woman's Journal* April 3, 1876, the sisters said that this "was utterly false, for he was trying a case in another part of the building. This Mr. Sumner heard the case for three days in the severity of winter, or pretended to do so, for some of the witnesses said that when the testimony on our side was before him, he generally turned to look out of the window; and we ourselves also observed it....Judge Sumner was employed in the lobby business in the case of our town versus Wethersfield, at the New Haven Assembly, which cost Glastonbury $2000., and there is no question in our mind that he was put on the bench as a contrived plan, as he would not dare to give the case against the town in favor of two defenseless women who had no vote." There is no way of determining whether the Smiths' charges were justified. Certainly, the ruling that there was no personal property was suspect. Ibid., 68.

Page 165, **WOMAN'S JOURNAL**

Ibid., 76.

Page 167, **WASHINGTON, D.C.**

Elizabeth Cady Stanton, Susan B. Anthony, Matilda Joslyn Gage, *History of Woman Suffrage, 1881-1887,* (Arno Press & The New York Times, 1969), 4.

Page 168, **HYMN**

Smith Papers, Historical Society of Glastonbury.

Page 169, **GRIEF**

In his *Autobiography and Reminiscences,* Henry Titus Welles said that Isabella Beecher Hooker attempted to convert Julia to spiritualism after Abby's death but to no effect. 84.

Chapter 11 -- A Bitter Epilogue

Page 170, **LETTER TO SUSAN B. ANTHONY**

Huntingdon Library, HM10567.

Page 172, **LETTER TO ISABELLA BEECHER HOOKER**

Smith Papers, Historical Society of Glastonbury.

Page 172, **OBITUARY**

Francis Ellen Burr had interviewed Julia and put in the obituary many of her remembrances which, although fascinating, were not completely accurate. For example, Julia told Burr she went to Emma Willard's school as a student when she was 20 years old which would have been in 1812. Actually she went in 1823 when she was 31 years old. So also she told Burr she had to attend dancing parties as a young woman because it was the only way she could stop being ridiculed for studying, a charge disproven by her own diary. She also told Burr that her parents gave up the farm in South Britain because her mother was totally unaccustomed to work of any kind, "least of all that of a farmer's wife," yet as has been shown, Hannah took an active role in running the Smith farm in Glastonbury, remaining physically active until the very end of her life.

Page 172, **PARKER'S APPEARANCE**

Katherine Hunt wrote "Although Miss Julia was the most intellectual and the finest scholar, she committed the greatest folly, that of marrying at the age of 87 an old fellow who by his own account was of great importance in his own state of New Hampshire, was not highly appreciated in his adopted home. He lived more than a century and his obituary said he had held more offices than any other men in his state. She seemed happy and proud of her conquest at first. Peace to his ashes." Mss, Henry Whitfield State Historical Museum, 8.

In an undated newspaper article titled "The Oldest College Graduate," is this description of Amos Parker. "Knowing that Mr. Parker is in his 99th year, one is puzzled to account for his crop of fine, brown hair. A wig, to be sure, but why brown? Simply because the wig was bought 50 or 60 years ago, when the wearer had a right to brown hair. Moreover, the color becomes him now. So much for the wig....He busies himself nowadays in reading and literary work, and in entertaining both friends and strangers with his vast store of recollections. As he boards the train he shows no sign of being unable to reach his Century mark." Smith Papers, Historical Society of Glastonbury.

See also Prudden, Historical Society of Glastonbury, 14.

Page 173, **LIVING WITHOUT STIMULANTS**

Letter to Isabelle Beecher Hooker, April 27, 1879, Smith Papers, Historical Society of Glastonbury, 3.

Page 173, **COURANT**

Smith Papers, Historical Society of Glastonbury.

Page 174, **DANCE OF BRIDE AND GROOM**

Kidder, Mss, Historical Society of Glastonbury, 21, 28.

Page 174, **RECEPTION**

Smith Papers, Letter to Isabella Beecher Hooker, Historical Society of Glastonbury.

Page 175, **PETITION**

Olive Rhines, "New Light on the Smith Story," *The Publick Post*, Winter, 1968.

Page 177, **PAYMENT OF TAXES**

Prudden, Historical Society of Glastonbury, 14.

Page 178, **BURR**

Stanton, *History of Woman Suffrage*, 334.

Page 178, **NOTE**

Burr Obituary, Smith Papers, Historical Society of Glastonbury.

Page 178, **WILL**

Newspaper Clippings, Smith Papers, Historical Society of Glastonbury.

Page 179, **LUCY STONE QUOTE**

Hale Memoir, Historical Society of Glastonbury, 12-13.

Page 180, **SCRIPTURE**

Smith Papers, Historical Society of Glastonbury, 204.

SELECTED BIBLIOGRAPHY

Ahlstrom, Sydney E. 1972. *A Religious History of the American People*. New Haven and London: Yale University Press.

Barber, John Warner. 1838. *Connecticut Historical Collections*. New Haven: Durrie & Peck.

Barbour Collection of Vital Records to 1850. Connecticut State Library, Hartford, Connecticut.

Barnes, Gilbert Hobbs. 1933. *The Antislavery Impulse, 1830-1844*. Gloucester, Mass.: Peter Smith.

Beman, Amos Gerry. Mss. Scrapbook. New Haven: Beineke Library, Yale University.

Berg, Barbara J. 1978. *The Remembered Gate: Origins of American Feminism: The Woman and the City, 1800-1860*. New York: Oxford University Press.

Brown, Barbara, James Rose. 1979. *Black Roots in Southeastern Connecticut, 1650-1900*. New London, Ct.: Gale Research Company.

Burr, Frances Ellen. undated. "Obituary of Julia Smith." Smith Papers, Historical Society of Glastonbury, Connecticut.

Cartledge, Pamela. 1987. "Seven Cows On The Auction Block: Abby and Julia Smith's Fight for Enfranchisement of Women." *The Connecticut Historical Society Bulletin* 52, no.1 (Winter): 15-43.

Chapin, Alonzo B. 1853. Reprinted 1976. *Glastenbury [sic] for Two Hundred Years 1853*. Hartford: Press of Case, Tiffany and Co.

Clay, Henry 1839. Speech. *Congressional Globe*, Appendix. Washington D.C.: U.S. Government Printing Office.

Conrad, Susan P. 1978. *Perish The Thought: Intellectual Women in Romantic America 1830-1860*. Secaucas, N.J.: The Citadel Press.

Cott, Nancy F. 1977. *The Bonds of Womanhood: "Woman's Sphere" in New England, 1780-1835*. New Haven and London: Yale University Press.

Craven, Avery. 1967. *The Coming of the Civil War*. New York: Harper and Row.

Dana. *Religious Organizations Collection.*, 1813-1949. Volume 119. New Haven Colony Historical Society.

Davis, Angela, Y. 1981. *Women, Race & Class*. New York: Vintage Books.

Dexter, Franklin Bowditch, ed., 1901. *The Literary Diary of Ezra Stiles*. Volume III. New York: Charles Scribner's Sons.

Donald, David. 1961. *Lincoln Reconsidered*. New York: Vintage Books.

Dubois, Ellen. 1979. "Women's Rights and Abolition: The Nature of the Connection." In *Antislavery Reconsidered: New Perspective on the Abolitionists*, eds. Michael Fellman and Lewis Perry. Baton Rouge and London: Louisiana State University Press.

Elkins, Stanley M. 1959. *Slavery: A Problem in American Institutional and Intellectual Life*. Chicago and London: The University of Chicago Press.

Fairfield East Association Records, Volume I. Archives, United Church of Christ Conference Center, Hartford, Connecticut.

Fairfield East Consociation Records, Volume I (1734-1813). Archives, United Church of Christ Conference Center,

Hartford, Connecticut.

--Anon. 1859. *Historical Sketch and Rules of Fairfield East Association and Consociation*. Archives, United Church of Christ Conference Center, Hartford, Connecticut.

Fellman, Michael, and Lewis Perry, eds. 1979. *Antislavery Reconsidered: New Perspectives on the Abolitionists*. Baton Rouge and London: Louisiana State University Press.

Filler, Louis. 1960. *The Crusade Against Slavery, 1830-1860*. New York: Harper Brothers.

Freehling, William W. 1990. *The Road to Disunion: Secessionists at Bay, 1776-1854*. Volume I. New York: Oxford University Press.

Friedman, Lawrence J. 1982. *Gregarious Saints: Self and Community in American Abolitionism: 1830-1870*. Cambridge: Cambridge University Press.

Friedman, Lawrence J. 1974. "Racism and Sexism in Ante-Bellum America: The Prudence Crandall Episode Reconsidered." *Societas*: 211-227.

Fuller, Andrew, Rev. 1852. *The Complete Works of Rev. Andrew Fuller: With a Memoir of His Life By Andrew Gunton Fuller*. Volume II. Philadelphia: American Baptist Publication Society.

Genovese, Eugene D. 1972. *Roll, Jordan, Roll: The World The Slaves Made*. New York: Vintage Books.

Gerteis, Louis S. 1987. *Mortality & Utility in American Antislavery Reform*. Chapel Hill and London: The University of North Carolina Press.

Glastonbury, Town Records. 1800-1835, transcription, Historical Society of Glastonbury, Connecticut.

--Records of Town Meetings 1862-77, 1877-1884, Town Hall,

Glastonbury, Connecticut.

--Electors' Meetings, 1838-1884, Town Hall, Glastonbury,
Connecticut.

Grant, Frederick C. 1961. *Translating The Bible*. Greenwich,
Connecticut: Seabury Press.

Graybill, Ronald D. 1987. "The Abolitionist-Millerite Connection."
In *The Disappointed*, eds. Ronald L. Numbers and Jonathan
M. Butler. Bloomington and Indianapolis: Indiana
University Press.

Green, Lorenzo Johnston. 1942. *The Negro in Colonial New
England 1620-1776*. New York: Columbia University Press.

Hale, J.H. Undated. "The Famous Smith Family of Glastonbury,
Conn." Mss., Smith Papers. Historical Society of
Glastonbury.

Halttunen, Karen. 1982. *Confidence Men and Painted Women: A
Study of Middle-class Culture in America, 1830-1870*. New
Haven and London: Yale University Press.

Hankins, Jean F. 1987. "A Different Kind of Loyalist: The
Sandemanians of New England During the Revolutionary
War." *New England Quarterly* LX, no. 2 (June): 223-249.

Hickok, David. Diaries 1769-79, Historical Society of Glastonbury.
Diaries 1771-1783, Connecticut State Library, Hartford,
Connecticut.

Housley, Kathleen L. 1988. "'The Letter Kills But the Spirit Gives
Life': Julia Smith's Translation of the Bible." *New England
Quarterly* LXI, no. 4 (December): 555-568.

Hunt, Katherine. Undated Mss. Curtesy of the Henry Whitfield State
Historical Museum, Guilford, Connecticut.

Hurd, D. Hamilton. 1881. *History of Fairfield County, Connecticut*.
Philadelphia: J.W. Lewis & Co.

Jensen, Joan M. 1986. *Loosening the Bonds: Mid-Atlantic Farm
Women, 1750-1850*. New Haven and London: Yale
University Press.

Jordan, Winthrop D. 1968. *White Over Black: American Attitudes
Toward the Negro, 1550-1812*. New York, London: W.W.
Norton & Co.

Judd, Wayne R. 1987. "William Miller, Disappointed Prophet." In
The Disappointed. eds. Ronald L. Numbers and Jonathan
M. Butler. Bloomington and Indianapolis: Indiana
University Press.

Kelley, Abigail Foster. Papers (letter from Hannah Smith to Abigail
Foster, 1839). Courtesy of the American Antiquarian
Society Worcester, Massachusetts.

Kidder, Mary Helen. 1937. "The Sisters Smith of Glastonbury:
Intellectuals, Rebels & Cranks." Mss. courtesy of the
Connecticut Historical Society, Hartford, Connecticut.

Kihn, Phyllis. 1969. "The Value Family of Connecticut." *The
Connecticut Historical Society Bulletin* 34, no. 3 (July): 79-
93.

Kingsley, William. ed. 1861. *Contributions To The Ecclesiastical
History of Connecticut*. New Haven: William L. Kingsley,
J.H. Benham, Printer.

Kraditor, Aileen, S. 1967. *Means and Ends in American Abolition*.
New York: Pantheon Books.

Logan, Gwendolyn Evans. 1965. "The Slave in Connecticut During
the American Revolution" in *Connecticut Historical Society
Bulletin*. 30, no. 3: 73-80.

Magdol, Edward. 1986. *The Anti-Slavery Rank and File, A Social
Profile of the Abolitionists' Constituency*. New York,
Westport, Ct., London: Greenwood Press.

McLoughlin, William G. 1959. *Modern Revivalism: Charles*

Grandison Finney to Billy Graham. New York: The Ronald Press Company.

McNulty, Marjorie Grant. 1983. *Glastonbury, From Settlement to Suburb*. The Historical Society of Glastonbury.

---1986. "Smith Sisters Revisited," *The Publick Post* 77 (Spring):1-6.

---1987. "Yale Classes Held Here in Revolutionary Wartime" in *The Publick Post* 78 (Spring-Summer): 1-4.

Morse, Jarvis Means. 1923. *A Neglected Period of Connecticut's History: 1818-1850*. New Haven, Ct.: Yale University Press.

Nichol, Francis D. 1945. *The Midnight Cry*. Washington, D.C.: Review and Herald Publishing Association.

Numbers, Ronald L. and Jonathan M. Butler, eds., 1987. *The Disappointed: Millerism and Millenarianism in the Nineteenth Century*. Bloomington and Indianapolis: Indiana University Press.

Parker, Wyman W. 1964. "The Jarvis Library." *Serif* 1, no. 2.

Prudden, Lillian E. 1949. Memoirs, Smith Papers, Historical Society of Glastonbury, Connecticut.

Purcell, Richard J. 1963. *Connecticut in Transition: 1775-1818*. Middletown, Connecticut." Wesleyan University Press.

Quarles, Benjamin. 1969. *Black Abolitionists*. New York: Oxford University Press.

Randell, James G. 1937. *The Civil War and Reconstruction*. Boston: D.C. Heath.

Record of Service of Connecticut Men in the War of the Revolution, 1889. Connecticut Adjutants General, Hartford, Connecticut.

Richard, Leonard L. 1979. "The Jacksonians and Slavery." In
  Antislavery Reconsidered: New Perspectives on the
  Abolitionists. Baton Rouge and London: Louisiana State
  University Press.

Rhines, Olive. 1968. "New Light on the Smith Story." *The Publick*
  Post 26 (Winter): 1-3. The Historical Society of
  Glastonbury, CT.

Roth, David M. 1979. *Connecticut: A History.* New York: W.W.
  Norton & Co. Inc.

Rowe, David L. 1985. *Thunder and Trumpets: Millerites and*
  Dissenting Religions In Upstate New York, 1800-1850.
  Chico, California: Scholars Press.

Sandeman, Robert. 1764. *Some Thoughts on Christianity in a Letter*
  To a Friend By Mr. Sandeman, Author of the Letters on
  Theron and Aspasio To Which is Annexed by Way of
  Illustration The Conversion of Jonathan the Jew As Related
  By Himself. Boston: W.M. Alpine and J. Flemming.
  Microfiche, Early American Imprints, American
  Antiquarian Society, Worcester, Massachusetts.

Sears, Clara Endicott. 1924. *Days of Delusion: A Strange Bit of*
  History. Boston and New York: Houghton Mifflin
  Company, The Riverside Press.

Sharpe, W.C. 1898. *South Britain Sketches and Records.* Seymour,
  Ct.: Record Print.

Sheldrick, Helen M., ed. 1971. *Pioneer Women Teachers of*
  Connecticut 1767-1970. Winsted, Connecticut:
  Dowd Printing Company.

Sklar, Kathryn Kish. 1973. *Catharine Beecher: A Study in American*
  Domesticity. New Haven and London: Yale University
  Press.

Smith, Abigail Hadassah. Letters, poems. Historical Society of
  Glastonbury, Connecticut.

Smith, Hannah Hadassah Hickok. Diary, account book, letters. Connecticut State Library, Hartford, Connecticut.

---1881. *Mother's Poems*. Hartford, Ct.: Press of the Case, Lockwood & Brainard Company.

---Undated. Translations. Historical Society of Glastonbury.

Smith, Julia E. 1877. *Abby Smith and Her Cows, with a Report of the Law Case Decided Contrary to Law*. Hartford: American Publishing Company.

---1810-1842. Diaries. Connecticut Historical Society. Hartford, Connecticut.

---1876. *The Holy Bible*. Hartford: American Publishing Company.

---1836-1856. Meteorological Journal. Connecticut Historical Society, Hartford, Connecticut.

Smith, Laurilla, Sketches. Smith Papers. Historical Society of Glastonbury.

Smith, Zephaniah. Letters, legal papers. Smith Papers. Historical Society of Glastonbury.

---Sermons. Mss, Archives. Connecticut Conference Center, United Church of Christ, Hartford, Connecticut.

Smith-Rosenberg, Carroll. 1985. *Disorderly Conduct*. New York and Oxford: Oxford University Press.

Speare, Elizabeth G. 1957. "Abby, Julia and the Cows." *American Heritage* 8, no. 4. (June): 54.

Sprague, William D., D.D. 1866. *Annual of the American Pulpit of Commemorative Notices of Distinguished American Clergymen of Various Denominations*. Volume I. New York: Robert Carter & Brothers.

Stampp, Kenneth M. 1956. *The Peculiar Institution: Slavery in the*

Ante-Bellum South. New York: Vintage Books.

Stanton, Elizabeth Cady, Susan B. Anthony, Matilda Joslyn Gage. 1881-87, reprinted 1969. *History of Woman Suffrage*. New York: Arno Press & The New York Times.

---1865. Letter to the Editor, *New York Standard*. December 26.

---1898. reprinted 1974. *The Woman's Bible*. Seattle: Coalition Task Force on Women and Religion.

Stern, Madeleine B. 1977. "The First Feminist Bible: The Alderney Edition, 1876." *Quarterly Journal of the Library of Congress* 34, no. 1: 23-30.

Stiles, Ezra, D.D. LL.D. Edited by Franklin Bowditch Dexter 1901. *The Literary Diary of Ezra Stiles, Volume III*. New York: Charles Scribner's Sons.

Strother, Horatio T. 1961. *The Underground Railroad in Connecticut*. Middletown, Ct. : Wesleyan University Press.

Swift, David E. 1978. *Sense of Mission, White and Black, in the Jacksonian Era: Willbur Fisk and Charles Ray*. Mss, Archives, Olin Library, Wesleyan University, Middletown.

---1989, *Black Prophets of Justice*. Baton Rouge and London: Louisiana State University Press.

deTocqueville, Alexis, 1835. Edited by John Stone and Stephen Mennell 1980, *On Democracy, Revolution and Society: Selected Writings*. Chicago and London: The University of Chicago Press.

Tyler, Alice Felt 1944. *Freedom's Ferment: Phases of American Social History to 1860*. Freeport, New York: Books for Libraries Press.

Tucker, Louis L. 1974. *Connecticut's Seminary of Sedition: Yale College*, Cheshire, Ct.: Pequot Press.

Van Dusen, Albert E., 1961. *Connecticut*, New York: Random House.

Walker, Peter F. 1978. *Moral Choices*. Baton Rouge and London: Louisiana State University Press.

Walker, Williston, 1901. "The Sandemanians of New England." *Annual Report of the American Historical Association.* Volume 1. Washington D.C.: 1902.,

Wayland, John. 1838. *The Limitations of Human Responsibility.* Boston: Gould, Kendell and Lincoln.

Webber, Thomas L. 1978. *Deep Like The Rivers: Education in the Slave Quarter Community, 1831-1865.* New York and London: W.W. Norton & Company.

Weisberger, Bernard H.; ed. 1963. *Abolition: Disrupter of the Democratic System or Agent of Progress?* Chicago: Rand McNally & Co.

Welles, Henry Titus 1899. *Autobiography and Reminiscences, Volume I.* Minneapolis: Marshall Robinson.

Wright, Joseph. Diary 1837-1863. Mss. The Historical Society of Glastonbury.

Yetman, Norman R. 1970, ed. *Life Under the "Peculiar Institution": Selections from the Slave Narrative Collection.* New York: Holt, Rinehart and Winston.

Zeicher, Oscar. 1949. *Connecticut's Years of Controversy: 1750-1776.* Chapel Hill: Published for the Institute of Early American History and Culture by the University of North Carolina Press.

Zilversmit, Arthur, Ed. 1967. *The First Emancipation: The Abolition of Slavery in the North.* Chicago and London: The University of Chicago Press.

INDEX

ABOUT THE AUTHOR

Kathleen Housley, a resident of Glastonbury, Connecticut, lives approximately a mile south of the Smith house. She has undergraduate and graduate degrees from Upsala College and Wesleyan University where she has been a teaching fellow in African American History and in Women's Studies. Her articles have appeared in *New England Quarterly, Journal of Negro History,* and *Christian Century.*